Testimony of YHWH's Word ©

Witnessed & Written

by

M L Helen Raphael BSc, MSc, MBACP

Testimony of YHWH's Word

ISBN: 978-1-910181-40-9

Published by Conscious Dreams Publishing

Dedication

To The Most Important People in my life…
My Darling Daughters Ria & Chane…
My Gorgeous 'Grandchis' Sian & Kal-El…
And to The Most Important Beings in my life…
YHWH my Father & my Messiah Yahsah!

"What a wonderful blessing to walk as a Child of YHWH... a calling I am proud to accept & share with the world.
Thank you my Father YHWH The Most High & my Messiah Yahsah for everything... including Your guidance in reading The Holy Scriptures... Your Sanctified Word... in a year!"*

* The Scripture readings are arranged chronologically in the order the historical events were believed to have taken place!

Foreword

I have truly come to know my Father YHWH The Creator of this universe and His Son The Messiah Yahsah; this book is a testimony of my walk with Them… and a true Testimony of YHWH's Word.

I have been on a journey to becoming a Child of YHWH since my acceptance of His calling 15 years ago. I didn't know Him as YHWH then… nor did I know His Son as Yahsah. However what I knew for sure is They existed and my desire was to get to know Them in search of my ultimate purpose in life. I made prayer for this desire based primarily on reading daily Scriptures… *"Ask & you will receive… seek & you will find… knock & it will be opened."* — **MATTHEW 7:7**. Well I asked and I definitely received… I searched and I certainly found… I knocked and it has surely been opened to me.

Along my initial journey I developed an essential spiritual habit of reading Scriptures daily encouraged by my brother in blood and spirit… a habit that has remained to this day in spite of reading through the entire bible three times to date.

I initially started my dedicated reading using the New King James Version. A few years later I was given a gift from my brother 'The Holy Word of YHWH'… a New World Translation of the bible exclusively made for me, bound in leather but most importantly with the replacement of the names Jesus, Jehovah, Lord and LORD with the true names of The Father and The Son… **יהוה** — YHWH pronounced YaHWaH — and **יהושע** — YHSH pronounced Yahsah. You see by this time I had been questioning concepts of the bible that the 'churches' were indoctrinating but just did not make sense to me or I just could not resonate with. The most prominent of these indoctrinations are the trinity and the traditional names of The Father and His Son.

When Angel Gabriel came to Mary and told her to name the child she was carrying... what name did he give her? It was certainly not Jesus... it could never have been as 1. Jesus is not a Hebrew name and 2. The letter J only came into existence in the 17th century. So if the name he gave was not Jesus then what was it? Yahsah is His Name taken from His Father's Name meaning = YAH is salvation... *"And you shall give birth to a Son and shall call His Name יהושע... for He shall save His People from their sins."* — **MATTHEW 1:21**. *"And when eight days were completed for Him to be circumcised His Name was called יהושע... the Name given by the messenger before He was conceived in the womb."* — **LUKE 2:21**

When Yahsah made prayer highlighted in JOHN 17 to whom was He speaking... Himself? When the voice out of Heaven spoke to John the Baptist as he was baptising Yahsah the Messiah saying... *"This is My Son The Beloved in Whom I delight."* — **MATTHEW 3:17**... Who was speaking and of Whom was He speaking? Yahsah to Himself... or YHWH of Himself? It doesn't make sense that They are the same beings as the trinitarian doctrine alludes to... and when those who attempt to indoctrinate use persuasive words as a means of casting away doubt such as "It's a mystery" I quote Yahsah's Words... *"Because it has been given to you to know the mysteries of the Kingdom of Heaven... but to them it has not been given..."* — **MATTHEW 13; 11**.

The trinity is undoubtedly a man-made doctrine of contriving error devised to deceive and lead YHWH's Children astray just as the false names of The Father and The Son are. We know that YHWH has an enemy and this enemy is also our enemy. His ultimate purpose is to annihilate the Children of The Most High. *"The thief does not come except to steal, to kill and to destroy".* Thank YHWH He gave us His Son as The Good Shepherd… *"I have come that they might possess life beyond measure… The Good Shepherd lays down His life for the sheep… but the one who does not own the sheep sees the wolf coming and leaves the sheep and flees… the wolf snatches the sheep and scatters them."* — **JOHN 10:10-12**.

So after many years of searching and researching in The Spirit of The Most High I have come to know the truth and through this testimony I want to share this truth with you. I now take my reading of Scriptures primarily from The Scriptures 2009 which uses an English translation of the Hebrew version of Scriptures keeping true to the Hebrew Names of The Father and The Son as well as all the prophets and other biblical greats. As Children of The Most High it is integral that we seek His Truth and Wisdom… ultimately it is essential for salvation.

"The fear of YHWH is the beginning of knowledge… If you seek her as silver and search for her as hidden treasures then you would understand the fear of YHWH and find the knowledge of El… for YHWH gives wisdom and out of His mouth comes knowledge and understanding." — **PROVERBS 1;7; 2:4-6**. *"For whatever is hidden shall be revealed… and whatever has been kept secret shall come to light… If anyone has ears to hear…let him hear."* — **MARK 4:22,23**.

I am living a truly simple life dedicated to doing what is right in the Eyes of The Almighty. I have encountered much negativity for my belief in the truth of YHWH and been viewed implicitly as insane, unstable or a heretic; not just from strangers but from friends and family alike just as Yahsah did. He spoke only truth yet His own people mocked, derided, rejected and ultimately murdered Him for it. There was a reason Yahsah preached the truth; to save souls because of His love for humanity. To believe in our Creator is to know He is real and understand that He has a purpose for our lives. That purpose is to be reconciled with Him who created us all… YHWH… so we may reside with Him and our Messiah in eternal love, peace and harmony. Yahsah came to the earth to do just that. I now know that my ultimate purpose is to help in this reconciliation process through witnessing the truth. It is both my privilege and joy to do so and this book is a tribute to my witness.

Within this book you will find three sections. The first section entails the 365 notes that I wrote daily after each reading of selected chapters enabling me to read the Holy Scriptures in one year. As highlighted they have been formatted in note and journal style edited only for grammar and spelling purposes so that the authenticity of my spiritual journey in the Scriptures remain. The table of contents lists the subtitles of each note and the scriptural readings for each day. The Scripture readings are arranged chronologically in the order in which the historical events were believed to have taken place.

The second section highlights the True Names of The Father and The Son with an extensive list of Scriptural verses referencing the importance of this knowledge. The third and final section gives a controversial yet accurate understanding of why the trinity is not of The Father; again with scriptural verses evidencing this fact.

I can only share what I know and this is what I know. I pray like me that you develop a daily habit of reading The Scriptures with dedication for the Truth of The Creator so you too can experience a life full of perfect wisdom, peace, love and longevity with The Father & The Messiah.

May YHWH bless and keep you till the day of rejoicing… where we as the Children of YHWH shall meet with Him and His Beloved Son as one… Amen!

"I do not pray for these alone but also for those believing in Me through their word so that they all might be one… as You Father are in Me and I in You so that they too might be one in Us so that the world might believe that You have sent Me." — JOHN 17:20,21.

"I am The Good Shepherd… I know Mine and Mine know Me… even as The Father knows me and I know The Father… I lay down My life for the sheep… And other sheep I have which are not of this fold I have to bring them as well… They shall hear My voice… and there shall be one flock… One Shepherd." — JOHN 10:14-16.

"יהושע exulted in The Spirit and said… 'I praise You Father… Master of the Heaven and the Earth… that You have hidden these matters from clever and learned ones and did reveal them to babes'… 'Father into Your Hands I commit My Spirit." — LUKE 10:21; 23;46.

Table of Contents

Day 1: The 1st day of the rest of my life...

Genesis 1, 2, 3

This is the beginning of my journey truly serving YHWH with full commitment... & how apt to start reading the Holy Scriptures from the beginning... the accounting of YHWH's creation of this Universe... Bless this journey Oh Father YHWH in an almighty way that every True Word of Yours remains indelibly printed in my heart, mind & soul... & on all those who have a sharing of this testimony... Amen!

Day 2: Continue on with YHWH...

Genesis 4, 5, 6, 7

So Cain killed Abel & YHWH destroyed the earth due to the wickedness of men... but He had a righteous man in Noah whom he saved along with his wife, sons and their wives... The rain caused a deluge for 150 days or 40... both these durations are documented... but the significance is not known at this present time... what is certain is that the righteous are saved... and through their obedience so are their families...

Day 3: I'm still moving...

Genesis 8, 9, 10, 11

I have read Genesis chapters 8, 9, 10 & 11... I was made aware of the nations that came from Ham, Shem & Japheth... & that Canaan the son of Ham was cursed due to Ham's disrespect of his Father Noah's drunken nakedness... YHWH makes a distinction in languages & Abraham's family leave Ur to go into the land of Canaan...

Day 4: Oh Job...

Job 1, 2, 3, 4, 5

Job had it all in the eyes of YHWH & all those around him… Satan with evil intent tested him… YHWH allowed it to prove Job's righteousness in Faith… But Job was so terribly afflicted & tormented he wished sincerely he hadn't been born cursing that day… how awful… Oh how this proves how much we MUST trust YHWH our El… He has promised to take care of us in every way & our El NEVER reneges on his promises… He chastises but only through love… He would not destroy His chosen, faithful & loyal Ones… or allow them to be destroyed… Amen!

Day 5: What a struggle...

Job 6, 7, 8, 9

Job is struggling in absolute torment... I too am struggling a little with confusion in things that Job is saying... but the Father is revealing what I need to know... Job is cursing the day he was born due to his excruciating pain & because he sees no hope he is asking YHWH to end his suffering by taking his life... He knows YHWH is the Almighty & the greatest of all but he is confused because he believes he must have sinned why this devastation has happened to him... & if he has why then is YHWH not revealing this to him... He has faith and knows YHWH is just & merciful but he so needs to express his pain & does so without cursing his El... He knows no man can ever be omnipotent, omniscience or omnipresent so continues to give glory to YHWH asking earnestly for His mercy...

Day 6: Heartfelt honesty...

Job 10, 11, 12, 13

Job was so pained and so confused which seemed to lead to anger... he had to get this off his chest and asked The Father what had he done... I imagine how I would feel having lost absolutely everything apart from my spouse... TRAUMATISED... Job knew he has been righteous but even then questioned himself because of the ginormous calamity that befell him... His friends we're not empathic nor understood... they 'played' at being faithful expressing their judgement of Job's expressions... Job was being real and honest with our Father YHWH but not irreverent or disrespectful... He was being like a true child with a father... one needing understanding through sufferance knowing that mercy and deliverance comes only from the Father...

Day 7: Job's torment & sorrow are deep...

Job 14, 15, 16

Oh my YHWH... Job is suffering tremendously... his friends lack empathy & are no comfort to him... Job pleads with You Father through his excruciating pain & You are merciful... He realises he is fallible & mortal... he knows You are the Most High & would never go against You... It seems his friends do not know You... they appear to be worshipping a hope of You & not the Counsellor in You... The One who understands we are of flesh & weak...

Day 8: Friends like these…

Job 17, 18, 19, 20

Who needs enemies when 'friends' like these exist? Job's friends have become like a curse to Him… likening him to the wicked with metaphorical examples of how the wicked will perish… It seems they believe that Job must have sinned why he is suffering so terribly… but Job is adamant he hasn't and that YHWH Almighty has delivered him to the wicked… However he is clinging on to hope as it is all he has… he says he may as well be dead otherwise… He also believes YHWH will redeem him… if he didn't he would most likely have taken his own life…

Day 9: Battle of understanding…

Job 21, 22, 23

Job had to contend with his friends who thought he was dishonouring YHWH… but it seems clear he wasn't & that his friends were lacking ability to comfort & support Job… Job was expressing the great pain of his torment but his friends were unable to empathise cause if they could surely they would understand his expressions were those of grief & traumatising pain… Thank You YHWH that You are understanding of the weakness of us in our flesh…

Day 10: Wisdom is key...

Job 24, 25, 26, 27, 28

Job continues to make expression of his grief and reflects on the wages of the wicked... Job evidently has a very close relationship with YHWH which is clear his friends do not... their worship appears legalistic and not through the Holy Spirit within... When does the Holy Spirit enter us? When we come to understand His Wisdom through the cleansing of the Word... JAMES 1 tells us this indubitably... Then we become more in harmony with the Ways of YHWH our Father... it is all written in His Word... simple...

Day 11: Job's reflections on righteousness...

Job 29, 30, 31

Job still contends with his losses & asks for answers from the Father... He believes he has walked righteously but asks YHWH that if he has sinned let it be known & let him be punished... Job speaks of the different ways sin could have occurred but is adamant he has not committed any... He feels YHWH has abandoned him & he is perplexed & terribly pained... yet he does not leave his faith because he knows YHWH is living & real... that He is the Almighty... & that if it were YHWH's will he could extinguish him... he knows YHWH has him... he knows YHWH will not let him down... he is just confused... & who wouldn't be in this situation... he has had to endured an atrocious situation but has not cursed The Most High once... he just wants to know why he has had to suffer in this way... I know it is Satan's doing... it seems that YHWH could rely on the faithfulness of Job to prove that Faith is alive in His children... YHWH promises He will never leave us nor forsake us... & Job knows this... so do I...

Day 12: **Elihu is tough on Job…**

Job **32, 33, 34**

It must have been so difficult for Job… I can only imagine how painful life was for him losing everything in the way he did… He was considered arrogant to believe he committed no sin… yet the opening chapters said just this… quite contradictory? So I guess really it is impossible for man not to sin… only Yahsah Messiah was perfect even in the flesh… however is it that Job was allowed to be tested by Satan because of imperfection? That his loss is a reminder of our fragility and frailty… and our constant need to come before YHWH for forgiveness with a desire to please him on a daily basis so our sins can be revealed to us? To be humble no matter what? Oh how difficult it is… but thank YHWH with Him it is possible…

Day 13: Elihu reprimands Job…

Job 35, 36, 37

Elihu though young but mature in wisdom humbles Job… he reminds him of YHWH's almightiness & the wondrous omnipotent things He does that no man can fully comprehend in this life… Elihu rebukes Job… I'm a little confused or maybe lacking understanding of Job's initial pleas to YHWH… I can imagine how awful it must have been for Job but I suppose Elihu is doing the best thing as a faithful loving brethren… he doesn't want Job to sin in his pain so brings to Job's mind the remembrance of YHWH's almightiness…

Day 14: YHWH finally answers Job...

Job 38, 39

YHWH is not best pleased with Job... He proceeds to enquire of Job how the entire planet & everything on it was formed... from the heavens, the galaxies, the elements, the animals, the measurements of all, the accuracy of timing in birth, precipitation, seasons etc... In other words we will only know a minute fraction of YHWH's thoughts & ways... therefore we cannot question them with arrogance... only with curiosity, intrigue, awe & humility...

Day 15: Job's beautiful new beginnings...

Job 40, 41, 42

YHWH reprimanded Job for his outburst... YHWH reminded him of His omnipotence & challenged Job to prove his own... but evidently Job is no match & quite rightly humbly accepted this... However YHWH rebuked his 3 friends for their lack of understanding & misguided information in spiritual matters... they were instructed to make offering to Job as an apology & to prove that Job was seen as righteous in YHWH's eyes... YHWH then rewarded & blessed Job more in the end than in his beginning... an ultimate evidence of patience and endurance... Amen!

Day 16: YHWH's true people...

Genesis 12, 13, 14, 15

Abraham is indeed the father of the nation chosen specially by YHWH... He was given the promise that his progeny will increase to a number innumerable to count... but even though he will have blessings of peace all his life & live to a good old age his descendants will suffer for 400 years by worldly rulers in the land of strangers due to their disobedience... is this particular time accounted in history a reference or symbolic to the slavery atrociously endured solely by descendants of an African race?

Day 17: Father of all nations...

Genesis 16, 17, 18

An eventful reading... Sara gives her maid Hagar to Abram to surrogate a child but Hagar ends up despising Sara... YHWH our Father comforts the maid Hagar when she is banished by Sara & promises that her son will be a leader of a blessed race... However YHWH's true covenant is with Abram who He renames Abraham & then gives a seed of the chosen nation to through Sarah who was also renamed... This was a true miracle as they were both very old and way passed child bearing age... however this makes the promise more pertinent that he shall give birth to YHWH's chosen nation Zion... Whilst this is happening Sodom & Gomorrah is to be destroyed... but on Abraham's plea YHWH saves his righteous... In the Scriptures we experience the first occurrence of circumcision & Abraham is instructed by YHWH to circumcise all who are in his household... those either by birth or bought...

Day 18: Posterity continues...

Genesis 19, 20, 21

From the destruction of Sodom & Gomorrah and the saving of Lot... through the impregnation of Lot's two daughters... to the saving of Hagar & her son Ishmael after Sarah banished them... YHWH expressed & kept the promise that Isaac shall be His chosen seed and that a great nation shall also come from Ishmael though he was half Egyptian but only because he is Abraham's seed... Progeny was preserved (albeit incestual according to today's society) in that Sarah was Abraham's half-sister... Lot fathered his two daughters' sons who became the nation of Moab & Ammon though Lot was unaware of the lurid act of copulation due to being deceitfully intoxicated by his daughters... YHWH's word is true & righteous & when He makes a promise He never fails... YHWH has made a beautiful planet & it's evident He has made it for habitation... habitation of a just, merciful & loving people...

Day 19: Sacrifices & blessings...

Genesis 22, 23, 24

YHWH never fails in His promises... He swore to Abraham He will bless him as a father of a great nation the number of which is greater than the stars in the universe & the grain of sands on the seashore... & so said so done... Abraham proved faithful to YHWH's word by preparing his son as a burnt offering on YHWH's instruction... of course YHWH saved his son... When Sarah finally expired a special field was bought for her burial & that of Abraham's family... he also sent his servant back to his country to seek a wife to comfort his son Isaac... Rebekah his great niece was chosen by YHWH through the prayers of both Abraham and his servant... So Bethuel, Rebekah's father, Laban her brother & Milcah her mother, on her acceptance sent her to her husband-to-be & their family with blessings that she may become the mother of a great nation who will be keepers of the gates of their enemies... again evidence of YHWH's promise of posterity...

Day 20: Jacob & Esau...

Genesis 25, 26

Abraham remarried & added another six sons to his lineage so had eight in total... but Isaac was the one given the chosen birth right though his brother Ishmael was also promised that a great nation would come from him... Rebekah gave birth to twins Jacob & Esau but the oldest sold his birth right for food... so it was the youngest who continued the progeny of Zion... Isaac was blessed mightily in the land of Gerar, the place they escaped to due to the famine... Abimelech saw the evident blessings of YHWH on Isaac and so asked for peace & forgiveness after he exiled Isaac due to his increased mightiness... Esau continued to bring grief to his parents by marrying out of his people... YHWH our El kept the promise despite the adversities experienced... Abraham's posterity grew truly giving birth to nation after nation...

Day 21: Blessings in deceit...

Genesis 27, 28, 29

Rebekah helped Jacob trick his father Isaac so that he may gain the blessings set aside for a 1st born Esau... but even when Isaac was made aware of the deceit he didn't take the blessing back... he did bless Esau but it remained, as providence would have it, that Esau the oldest would serve his brother Jacob the youngest... so now it makes sense... YHWH had instructed Rebekah to dress Jacob as Esau... So Jacob was sent away to his mother's people to find a wife as Rebekah abhorred the thought of him marrying from the Hittites... He was given both the elder & the younger daughters of Laban, Leah & Rachel, for whom he worked 14 years to gain... he was tricked into marrying Leah because she was the 1st born & it was customary... but Laban kept his promise & gave Rachel, the one whom Jacob loved the most... YHWH was kind to Leah and allowed her to bear Jacob four sons... the 1st four of the Twelve Tribes of Israel...

Day 22: Oh to be blessed by YHWH…

Genesis 30, 31

When YHWH says He will bless you then He surely will… However those blessings are contingent to our faith & righteousness… the only way of knowing how to exact these is through the reading of Scriptures… Jacob was truly blessed with twelve sons, one daughter, two wives, two concubines, livestock & servants… Laban, his father-in-law was blessed as a result but tried to deceive him… again the blessings of The Father being with Jacob meant he was protected & Laban lost out instead… Thankfully the peace of Jacob & the protection of YHWH meant Laban could see his wrong & asked for a peaceful covenant… Amen to YHWH & his righteous!

Day 23: Reunions & retributions...

Genesis 32, 33, 34

Jacob left his father to escape the wrath of Esau after deceiving him out of his birth right & blessings.... he had been gone more than 14 years before he made the decision to return to the land YHWH gave him & make reconciliation with his twin Esau... Jacob fearing Esau still had anger towards him made contingencies... he showered him with gifts of animals but not before wrestling with The Father & requesting a blessing which he received... Wrestling with YHWH? What did this mean? According to Scriptures Jacob had the power to restrain Him... how? I'm sure it was an Angel of YHWH... but why? Anyway Jacob settled in the land of Canaan where his only daughter suffered a rape but was requested as a wife by her rapist Shechem & his father... Jacob consented on the proviso that they & all their people were circumcised & followed their faith... they agreed & were circumcised only to be killed in their weakened state immediately following circumcision by Levi & Simeon bringing shame & disrepute to Jacob who had to make plans to leave the land lest he & his people were slayed...

Day 24: Jacobs sons...

Genesis 35, 36, 37

Jacob... now called Israel (meaning he wrestled with El)... was constantly reminded by YHWH that he would be father to nations & that kings would come forth from him & so said so done... his sons are the Twelve Tribes... his brother Esau was father of the Edomites & many other huge nations... & his uncle Ishmael father to the Ismaelites... Rachel died giving birth to Benjamin, Israel's last born & his sons sell Joseph to Ismaelites as a slave... thank YHWH Reuben saved him from being murdered by his brothers... Joseph was given the gift of dreams & interpretation & when he dreamt his brothers, his father & mother would bow down to him his brothers were incensed and infuriated... they already had animosity towards him because he was favoured most by his father... jealousy truly got the better of them leading to evil thoughts and evil deeds... but YHWH remained with him saving him from death... however poor Jacob... his soul was tortured by the thought of his son mauled & ripped apart by an animal because his sons brought back this lie along with the coloured coat he had made for Joseph shredded & covered in goat's blood to further corroborate their deceit...

Day 25: YHWH is merciful…

Genesis 38, 39, 40

How strange and wonderful it is to understand the Scriptures… Tamar lost her 1st husband, Judah's 1st son Er due to his wickedness… but she wanted a son & Judah wanted an heir so gave his 2nd son as a husband… but his son felt cheated & dropped his sperm so she wouldn't conceive… YHWH also destroyed him as a result… Judah's youngest was promised to her when he grew but that didn't take place either… so when she disguised herself as a harlot Judah took her in his grief as a widow & she became pregnant… Judah heard & wanted her burned to death but she proved that it was him that fathered her… he indeed admonished her righteous act and so too did YHWH… I suppose those days were different to ours… would Judah's act of sleeping with a harlot be acceptable… or Tamar's by sleeping with her father-in-law? Incest & inter-breeding as it's referred to today seemed acceptable in those days… Then we read about Joseph's tribulation & the Father constantly with him granting him favour in the eyes of his masters so he was given great positions of trust… even when he was sent to jail on the lie of his master Potiphar's wife, mercy & favour continued to follow him… so too the gift of dream interpretation… When YHWH is for you who can be against you?

Day 26: Joseph's redemption...

Genesis 41, 42

What an almighty El YHWH of Israel is... Joseph dreamt of his future leadership but was rebuked, physically abused & sold as a slave when he recounted his dream to his brother's... But after all Joseph experienced it lead him to be the most powerful governor in Egypt 2nd only to Pharaoh... again because of his gift of dreams & interpretation... How wonderful for his father, brothers & family because he was now in the position to maintain their lives in the midst of the 7-year famine... but not without his brothers suffering emotional torment & guilt & their father Jacob reliving the pain of losing his son & further fear of losing another...

Day 27: The beautiful reconciliation...

Genesis 43, 44, 45

I have always loved this as one of my favourite scriptural accounts... Joseph in his humility, total wisdom & understanding... he recounts the dream & understands that what his brothers did in enslaving him to Egyptians was predestined so he could be lifted up to his majestic position to continue the promise of posterity granted to Abraham, Isaac & Jacob... Joseph demonstrates complete faith in love & humility... absolutely wonderful, edifying, inspiring & exemplifying witness...

Day 28: Family unity...

Genesis 46, 47

The beauty & strength of family bonding & togetherness... Joseph had been lifted into high status & due to this fact during the famine he could offer his family vital refuge with Pharaoh's blessings... imagine seventy members of Jacob's flesh & blood relocated to Goshen in Egypt... his twelve sons, one daughter, fifty-four grandchildren & four great grandchildren... resettled together as a whole family... carrying each other's trials, pains, joys & duties... sticking together through thick & thin due to blood & kinship... These scriptures demonstrate the way our Father wants us to be... but not just for sake of kinship by blood but kinship through spirit & faith... because in this day that's what family is... those doing the will of YHWH... blood or water...

Day 29: Jacob blesses his sons...

Genesis 48, 49, 50

Jacob knowing he was about to die gave separate blessings to each one of his twelve sons & to Joseph's two sons which he called his own... he informed Joseph that the next offsprings he has will be his own & they shall serve Ephraim the youngest 1st then Manasseh... Jacob blessed his sons according to their indiscretions but Judah & Joseph received the greatest of the blessings with Reuben, Simeon & Levi receiving the worst due to their violence & wicked deeds... So Jacob was buried in the land YHWH promised and as requested in the burial place in the cave of Machpelah where Abraham, Sarah, Isaac, Rachel & Leah were also buried... He was mourned 70 days in Egypt & 7 days in Canaan with great & solemn lamenting... His sons feared Joseph would avenge their wickedness but Joseph wept & promised he would take care of them & their families... and so said so done... Joseph saw three generations of his offspring & he died at the ripe old age of 110 years in Egypt...

Day 30: Moses…

Exodus 1, 2, 3

Joseph passes away and in time so too the then king of Egypt… So the new king that reigns who has no direct knowledge of Joseph decides the Hebrews are too big & fearful as a race… in attempting to overpower them the king enslaves them & orders the boy babies to be destroyed at birth to keep the rate of the Hebrew race from further increasing… Now Moses… a Hebrew baby of the Levi tribe… was hidden in the Nile & found by Pharaoh's daughter… he was raised an Egyptian but killed an Egyptian so exiled himself to Midian… He married Zapporah, Jethro Reuel's daughter… whilst in Horeb in the mountain of El, YHWH spoke to him his mission that he was to lead YHWH's people out of the land of Egypt into the land of milk & honey… Canaan… Moses was perplexed thinking how would a lowly person like him have power to give command to Pharaoh… but YHWH assured him He would be with him every step of the way to empower & deliver him & his people… YHWH gives grace & life to all those who exercise faith in Him…

Day 31: YHWH's power in Moses...

Exodus 4, 5, 6

So Moses the great great grandson of Jacob from the tribe of Levi saw himself as illiterate & uneducated (with possibly a speech impediment) so could not understand how or why YHWH chose him to lead Zion YHWH's people away from Pharaoh... out from Egypt into Canaan... & how he would get both the Israelites or Pharaoh to heed his words... But YHWH is the Almighty & nothing is impossible with Him... He can make anything happen... I struggled at first to understand what was meant by "YHWH hardens Pharaoh's heart"... why would YHWH want to... but look how the power of pray is real... I prayed for understanding & wisdom & was given understanding... Pharaoh the King like all powerful men in the world have huge egos... he serves his own false god... through idolatrous worship, money, materialism & self-exultation... so when Moses tells him to release YHWH's people so they may serve & worship their El, Pharaoh is incensed because of his own self-importance & arrogance so does not accept this command but hardens his heart even more & increases the punishment of YHWH's children even more... YHWH does not directly harden his heart... his heart becomes hardened and cold due to his self-conceited goals... but YHWH says to Moses not to give up or give in giving him his brother Aaron as his spokesman & emotional support...

Day 32: Pharaoh's hardened heart...

Exodus 7, 8, 9

What makes a man believe he is greater than YHWH the True El... Creator of this Universe... Supreme Ruler... the Most High? YHWH made Moses a god & Aaron his brother a prophet to him so when they went up against Pharaoh the Power of YHWH would be apparent... more so than Pharaoh's magicians & sorcerer's... yet Pharaoh still continued to harden his heart... why? Because his desirous intent was wicked... & as human's we are led by the desires of our heart... "Where our heart is there also our treasures will be"... Imagine through all the disasters that struck Pharaoh & his Egyptians... completely by-passing the Israelites... Pharaoh still didn't heed or care about his people... he would rather remain stubborn & that they suffer & die than to give them freedom... he believed he was greater than YHWH despite the evidence to the contrary... he contended with The Most High in his deceit, arrogance & malice delusionally believing he was going to win... he was blinded & made foolish by his lack of humility and therefore was to pay the ultimate price... Satan evidently led him by the desires of his heart...

Day 33: The Exodus of Zion…

Exodus 10, 11, 12

"Those who are humble I shall exalt… & those who are arrogant I shall humble & humiliate"… Those are the words of YHWH certainly in the case of Moses & Pharaoh… Pharaoh was such a stubborn man that he & his people suffered terribly… Moses in his humility & obedience was delivered in greatness by YHWH… The Law of the Passover was set in regulation & after 430 years from the days of Joseph the Israelites finally left Egypt with their El YHWH in front of them & behind them taking care of them & the strangers amongst them who also heeded His laws & regulations…

Day 34: YHWH's Victory over Pharaoh...

Exodus 13, 14, 15

Pharaoh was so hard-hearted & stubborn it completely blinded his judgement... causing him to be destroyed along with a complete annihilation of his army depicted in the magnificent miracle of the parting of the Red Sea... However no matter how much the Israelites witnessed in terms of YHWH's miraculous powers their faith still diminished when they were faced with troubles & dilemmas... What does it really take to have faith? Moses exemplified true faith... so too his siblings...

Day 35: Israelites lack faith...

Exodus 16, 17, 18

Oh what a complaining people the Israelites were despite all that YHWH had done... they were afflicted in Egypt & called out to Him for help... He delivered them & promised them a new, flourishing land... He fed & watered them but yet their complaints never ceased... they forgot so quickly the Works of YHWH in response to their fleshly desires... They had no impulse control & were continually wanton & greedy... even when YHWH provided Manna at dawn & quail at night they still stocked up when He said not to making the extra food rot with worms... A stubborn, hard of hearing, selfish & ungrateful people that when they complained to Moses he reminded them their complaints were actually to YHWH... A blessing for Moses was his father-in-law Jethro's guidance in the skill of management and the art of delegation which helped to increase peace & endurance for Moses and gave responsibility & ownership to the people... all with the blessings of YHWH...

Day 36: The Ten Commandments...

Exodus 19, 20, 21

These Ten Commandments are indelibly written & no blotting out or erasing of them shall ever take place... The times before Yahsah our Messiah, sacrificial laws & statutes were set that meant on a regular basis these had to be adhered to... but when Yahsah came as the ultimate sacrifice once for all time these sacrificial laws were done away with... all but the Ten Commandments... would YHWH say it's ok to kill, steal or lie? The truth lies in faith... that when we truly believe YHWH is real... that He sent His Son to redeem His people... cleanses our sins & reconciles us to Him... then we will naturally & gradually do that which pleases Him because we have become our true selves... those born of the Most High...

Day 37: YHWH reveals Himself & His Laws...

Exodus 22, 23, 24

Yes, YHWH gave Moses to be leader over His people & as such revealed all the laws pertaining to everyday living as well as The Ten Commandments... He then instructs that they keep 3 feasts for the year... The Feast of Unleaven... the Feast of Harvest... & the Feast of Ingathering... YHWH then invited Moses, Aaron, Nadab, Abihu (Aaron's two sons) & seventy Elders to join Him on the Mount of Sinai where they saw YHWH standing on a paving of sapphire... there they ate & drank in the presence of YHWH... what an honour... but then Moses was requested to spend 40 days alone with YHWH to conclude the Laws which YHWH wrote on tablets... Moses was such an obedient & devout Child of YHWH... He took his leadership seriously with humility, loyalty & love... He read to the people from the Book of the Covenant & made confessions & sacrifices on their behalf...

Day 38: Spectacular Tabernacle & Ark...

Exodus 25, 26, 27

Wow... how beautiful the Ark, the Mercy Seat, the Tabernacle, the lamp stand, the table & utensils must have looked... the workmanship of wood, gold, silver, bronze, fine linen & silk embroidery... The task of producing these was given to Moses & the role of priestly duty given to Aaron & his sons by YHWH... What an honour to be chosen by YHWH to do a fine works or to lead... knowing your true role in life pertaining to YHWH is peace giving & truly purposeful... this is where I want to be...

Day 39: YHWH's Holy Ordination...

Exodus 28, 29

So YHWH ordained Aaron & his sons to minister specifically to Him... He instructed Moses to have priestly garments made specifically for them... the ephod & breastplate for Aaron & tunics for his son made of the finest linen, threads, gold & precious stones... These are YHWH's inanimate creations used without ego to His glory... to be admired as such but not to be used in greed or for egotistical status... The sacrifice of the animals was also very specific... for heave, sin, peace, grain, drink & burnt offering... & for bodily sustenance for Aaron & his sons only after Moses performed the Holy consecration instructed by our Father YHWH...

Day 40: **Sacrifice & sin...**

Exodus **30, 31, 32**

Imagine Moses spent 40 privileged days with the Father on Mount Sinai being instructed with the Laws of Commandments & Sacrifices... including the making of anointing oil & incense... & the names of YHWH's men whom He gave the gift to produce the artistic works... But the Israelites waiting below became impatient & already tempted Aaron to build an idol of gold to worship... which he did... YHWH knew this took place & in his anger against their sin swore to destroy them... but Moses in his love for the people & for his El YHWH entreated YHWH not to as he believed the Egyptians would believe YHWH to be a cold and cruel El who took His people out of Egypt only to kill them... So YHWH spared their lives due to Moses... however when Moses himself came down from the mountain & saw the people worshipping & celebrating the false god... the golden calf... he truly understood the anger of YHWH & commanded that those on YHWH's side kill their brother, companion & neighbour who were not... So said so done... YHWH made an oath that those who sinned by turning to a false god would be blotted out of His Book of Life... what did these people really need to hear or see for them to keep their faith in YHWH? They were so fickle, stubborn & foolish... they were so ungrateful & blind... this cost them their lives... & ultimately their souls...

Day 41: YHWH renews His Covenant...

Exodus 33, 34, 35

Moses was so special in YHWH's Eyes that he was able to persuade YHWH to return amongst His people & renew the Covenant... He rewrote the Commandments on new stones & had regular meetings with Moses... Moses shone with His glory every time they met & all the people could see... As an acceptance of the Covenant the people donated with willing hearts all that YHWH instructed so that all the Holy articles could be made... He gave wisdom & skill to the artisans... These are all the things possible with YHWH... He can excel the mind so that anything man does is possible with Him... Amen!

Day 42: The artisans at work...

Exodus 36, 37, 38

How stunning the tabernacle & it's furnishings, the Ark & the mercy seat, & all the utensils for service must have looked... nothing but the best materials of gold, silver, bronze, acacia wood, fine linen & silk threads used... It really evidences that the things of YHWH are all good & come in abundance... the Israelites donated so much that Moses had to tell them to stop... there was literally an overwhelming amount of gifts... that's how YHWH works... then the work of the artisans with their amazing skills & intricate artistry... What a spectacular sight it must have been to behold...

Day 43: Beautiful & Holy...

Exodus 39, 40

Aaron & his son's garments were the last to be made & how absolutely splendid they must have been... thread made of real gold... precious stones set within the garments representing each of the Twelve Tribes... & beautiful embroidered pomegranates with magnificent gold bells set between them on the hem... WOW... Moses was certainly most special in the Eyes of YHWH... He was made overseer of all the works for ministry & to ensure the progress of ministry to YHWH during the whole journey of their exodus... what an honour & a privilege...

Day 44: YHWH's sacrificial offerings...

Leviticus 1, 2, 3, 4

So here we understand the different offerings on the altar to YHWH... burnt... grain... peace... & sin offerings... using lamb... bull... goat... turtle doves... & pigeons... different preparations... sexes... & animals for the different offerings... but all include the use of blood as the atonement for forgiveness as well as the demonstration of thankfulness... These rituals were a significant part of the ways of the Israelites as instructed by YHWH... who could know the mind of YHWH & His full understanding concerning these things? Obedience... faith... humility... & trust comes to my mind...

Day 45: Sacrificial laws continue...

Leviticus 5, 6, 7

Moses continued to explain the processes of each sacrificial offering to Aaron the chosen priest... to his sons the chosen ministers... & to the rest of the Israelites... these processes were all specific & explicit & in themselves if broken would impute further sin leading to excommunication...

Day 46: Aaron's priestly duties begin...

Leviticus 8, 9, 10

So all the preparation of the building of the tabernacle, designing of the utensils & the priestly robes & the instruction of the sacrificial offerings has now finally given way to the start of Aaron & his sons ministry to YHWH... Aaron & his sons were consecrated by Moses in a 7-day ritual that meant they could not leave the tabernacle... if they did it would be fatal for them... They then performed the sacrificial offerings on behalf of themselves & their people as Moses had instructed on behalf of the Father YHWH... & as promised YHWH presented Himself to them all... But Aaron's sons Nadab & Abihu went on their own volition to offer profane fire to YHWH & perished as a punishment... The people fell prostate on YHWH's appearing... The rituals that YHWH set were to be followed perfectly & woe to any who disobeyed or dismissed them... Today all we have to do as YHWH's people is exercise faith in His Son Yahsah our Messiah as He became the ultimate sacrificial lamb once and for all mankind... We no longer have to follow those rituals... following Yahsah's ways & His mind is our only requirement & we have help always thru the request of the Holy Spirit... the desire of our heart is where we start!!

Day 47: Rituals of living continued...

Leviticus 11, 12, 13

Moses continues to give the Israelites more laws & rituals concerning their existence... those relating to clean & unclean foods... what is & isn't permitted to be eaten... the ritual for the woman after giving birth & those concerning leprosy... YHWH was very specific regarding these rituals... isn't it bizarre that for many in the world these rituals still continue even though they bear no significance to YHWH anymore... He has made it more simple & less ritualistic to enter righteousness... but many have been misguided in their faith because they are not themselves searching for the Truth but relying on others to do it for them..."many will perish from lack of knowledge"...

Day 48: Biological uncleanness...

Leviticus 14, 15

Leprosy was an awful disease spoken throughout scriptures... YHWH set rituals for the priests in how to cleanse anyone or anything contaminated with leprosy... The blood of the trespass offering was placed on the tip of the right ear... the thumb of the right hand & the big toe of the right foot... on top of this the oil offered for atonement was placed... I'm intrigued as to why these 3 places on the body... Women menstruating where considered unclean... so too anything they were in contact with... she had to also give offering 7 days after it stopped... 2 turtle doves or young pigeons were to be given as sin & burnt offerings... Men would have to do the same if they suffered discharge... If they had released semen in copulation they were unclean until sunset...

Day 49: Atonement... scapegoat... lifeblood & sexual morality...

Leviticus 16, 17, 18

Moses was regularly instructed by YHWH just as a king or president... he had the duty of the 1st Commander so to speak... These were the times before Yahsah our Messiah & as such one specific day a year had to be dedicated to atoning of sins initiated as an everlasting statute by Aaron... the 7th month on the 10th day... YHWH revealed the blood as the life source and as such forbade anyone to eat of it or they would be cut off... blood was only ever to be used for cleansing and atonement for sin... Sexual immorality & indecency was rife around Canaan... YHWH commanded His people to stay away from these abominable ways to prevent being cut off from Zion... no revealing the nakedness of family... no bestiality... no sexual acts with the same sex... YHWH was very clear of the preservation of nature as He intended and gives an understanding that the dark spirits infiltrate the mind to behave in a way that is contrary to nature...

Day 50: Moral conduct...

Leviticus 19, 20, 21

Well YHWH set the laws for moral conduct & anyone who didn't follow them were either cut off or destroyed... Incest, homosexual acts, Molech worshipping, prostitution, adultery, bestiality & fortune telling are all an abomination to YHWH and punishable by death... YHWH can only be associated with holiness... not even a blemished person could minister as priest within The Most Holy of the tabernacle... but it didn't mean he couldn't minister at all... Other laws were administered.... no tattoos, giving harvest food to the poor, honouring parents, not stealing or lying, being just & honourable, not hating or holding grudges & not mistreating strangers... these were some of the laws set by YHWH... Question: Is a blemished individual considered a curse?

Day 51: The Feasts of YHWH...

Leviticus 22, 23

So YHWH declared to Moses all the feasts that should be celebrated throughout the year... the Sabbath, the Passover, the Unleaven Bread, the Firstfruits, the Weeks, the Trumpets, the Day of Atonement & the Tabernacles... many of the feasts took place in the seventh month... the Israelites were given 'bank holidays' to give full credence to these feasts which when followed promoted blessings for Zion... when we give righteously to YHWH He gives back mightily that "there is not room enough to receive it"... all praises to YHWH The Almighty...

Day 52: The Laws continued...

Leviticus 24, 25

YHWH continues to instruct Moses of more laws that Moses must in turn inform the people of... As for Aaron he is further in charge of caring for the precious tabernacle lamps & preparation of the 12 show breads... Blaspheming the name of YHWH is punishable by death... in those days they were stoned... now it would mean being written out of the Book of Life... Death was considered a necessity & had a different interpretation to now... YHWH is in charge of life & death... but after Yahsah came life... & death took on new meaning it seems moving from the sacrificial fleshly form to a faithful spiritual form... YHWH always took care of His people... & will always continue to take care of us... The law of Jubilee & Sabbaths meant blessings in produce & redemption from slavery or hired service... also a reconciliation to one's family or land...

Day 53: **Promises or die...**

Leviticus **26, 27**

After YHWH had instructed Moses with all the commandments, statutes & laws YHWH then instructed Him with what would happen if these were blatantly not adhered to... every blessing would be removed & every generation would suffer the retribution of their father's iniquities unless they confess these & their unfaithfulness by humbling & accepting the guilt... Imagine now how people refuse to believe there is an Almighty El... & even those who say they believe they have their own twisted ideas of who He is & who they themselves are...

Day 54: The 1st ever census...

Numbers 1, 2

On the 2nd of Iyyar (Ziv) in the 2nd year of the Exodus the very 1st census was commanded by YHWH... those numbered were only men over 20 years and fit for war... separated by their tribes... Joseph's was split between Ephraim & Manasseh... & the tribe of Levi were not counted as they were given charge of the Tabernacle of the Testimony... The tribes were positioned specifically in camps on each of the compass points with the Tabernacle & the Levite tribes directly in the middle... no one else was allowed to take charge of the Tabernacle except the Levites lest they perished... 603,550 in all was the total of males 20 years+ of strength to soldier... YHWH set leaders over each tribe... imagine these were all from Jacob's seeds...

Day 55: Levites duties...

Numbers 3, 4

The Levites were the only tribe not numbered for fighting duties... YHWH had sanctified them for duties pertaining to the Tabernacle... all males from the age of 30-50 years performed duties from the tribes of Gershon, Kohath & Merari... these were Aaron's sons... they were each given specific tasks to perform when moving from camp to camp... the Kohathites were given duties in the Most Holy that only they were to do lest anyone else would perish... Of all the 1st born of the rest of the Israelites 5 shekels was redeemed for each & the total amount given to Aaron & his sons...

Day 56: Law of jealousy & the Nazarite Law...

Numbers 5, 6

If a man was jealous towards his wife with good reason or not she was taken to the priest & tested by drinking bitter water... If she sinned her fertility would cease... If not it would remain intact... The Nazarite Law disallowed any consumption from the vine... even contact with the dead was not permitted... They would grow their hair but this would be shaved if they violated the Nazarite Law... They would however have opportunity to make good through burnt, sin, peace & grain offering as signifies the 'Law of Separation'... Many rituals & processes of offerings that were explicitly specified had to be made... but were not permanent or absolute... That's why they were done away with when Yahsah gave Himself to be the ultimate sacrifice... simple really!!

Day 57: The 1st offering for Levitical work...

Numbers 7

The time had come after the completion of the Tabernacle for the appointed leaders of the Twelve Tribes to make their offering to the Tabernacle work of the Levitical priest over a 12-day period... a day for each leader to make his offering with the tribe of Judah offering first... When the offering days were complete YHWH spoke with Moses from above the Mercy Seat situated above the Ark... The tribes truly took care of all their needs... spiritual & otherwise... under the guidance of Moses as instructed by our Father YHWH...

Day 58: YHWH leads by cloud & fire...

Numbers 8, 9, 10

YHWH instructs Moses to sanctify the Levites to Him... no longer are the 1st born of Israel to be set apart... Then He instructs the Israelites always through Moses to follow the cloud... when it is still over the tabernacle they remain encamped... when it moves they restart their sojourn... 2 trumpets were ordered to be hammered out in silver... they were to sound at various times... when all had to come before the tabernacle... when only the leaders were to come... when enemies approached... when they were heading out from camp etc... The Passover ceremony was still to be kept by all... strangers & natives alike... It was certainly a time of true collectiveness for YHWH's people & for the strangers amongst them... obedience was integral for protection & sustainment of life...

Day 59: Trials & blessings...

Numbers 11, 12, 13

As was their custom now the people continued to complain... this time they wanted meat even though YHWH sent manna everyday... Moses unfortunately was overwhelmed from carrying their burden so YHWH transferred some of the responsibility to 70 elders that YHWH told him to choose... Our Father YHWH sent thousands of quail for the people but consumed those who moaned with fire... Then Miriam was plagued with leprosy as she & her brother Aaron judged Moses for marrying an Ethiopian woman... however at the plea of Aaron to Moses & Moses to YHWH she was healed 7 days later after being sent away from the camp... Spies were then sent to recce the land YHWH promised them... to seek how the soil was... the strength of the peoples... the produce... the buildings etc... Giant people of Anak were observed & the soil & it's produce of good quality... The spies observed that indeed this land was truly of milk & honey...

Day 60: Disobedience, selfishness, weakness...

Numbers 14, 15; Psalms 90

Oh how YHWH must have been so disappointed & hurt... He saved His people from Egypt's wrath of slavery & was taking them into the Promised Land... yet for all the miracles He performed to keep them fed, housed, clothed & protected the Israelites never ceased with their complaints & disrespect... Therefore although Moses pleaded for YHWH's mercy YHWH destroyed those who rebuked Him including 2 of the 4 men sent out as spies... Caleb & Joshua were the other 2 that He saved for they remained loyal & faithful just as Moses... Psalms 90 is said to be Moses' prayer of thankfulness & praise to YHWH for all He had done from the beginning of time...

Day 61: What insolence & arrogance...

Numbers 16, 17

My goodness... what a people that were so ungrateful full of big egos & blind to YHWH's blessings... YHWH chose Moses & Aaron to lead the Israelites & the priesthood respectively...YHWH had delivered His people from Egypt but this was still not enough for those stiff-necks... Moses then put a test to these rebels resulting in YHWH consuming Korah & his whole family... women & children alike... they were swallowed up by the earth... He also consumed the other revolters who went up against Moses... 250 men in all... YHWH then commanded that all 250 censers that was burning the incense be remoulded into a bronze hammered plate for the alter as a sign... Yet again the peoples complained & blamed Moses for these men & Korah's family perishing... so YHWH sent a plague... had it not been for Moses pleading with Aaron to make atonement there would've been more than the 14,700 Israelites who perished... YHWH allowed only Aaron's rod to blossom buds, flowers & ripened almonds above the leaders of the other Twelve Tribes making the people fearful... It must be that other signs & wonders aside from YHWH's was taking place... why else would the people revolt against Him not accepting all the blessings He performed for them as Holy & True?

Day 62: **Levites blessings...**

Numbers **18, 19, 20**

Only Levites were allowed to minister in the Tabernacle to YHWH... therefore they had no land as inheritance & the 10% given as tithes to YHWH by the Israelites went to the Levites... the Levites had to give 10% of this to YHWH including all choice animals, grain & produce... nothing but the best for the Levites & for YHWH... It was in Meribah that Aaron & Moses lost their rights to enter the Promise Land... the Israelites complaints got too much for them that they sinned by not exposing YHWH's blessing to quench the thirst of his people... YHWH also informed Aaron of his imminent death... & so Moses had to prepare Aaron's son as his heir to the priesthood... This is indication that YHWH does let His children know their time of passing...

Day 63: Power of YHWH...

Numbers 21, 22

The Father blesses those who are obedient in faith... Israel defeated their neighbours so they could claim the land... all those who complained YHWH sent serpents to kill them... Moses pleaded on behalf of those who were sorry so YHWH instructed him to make a bronze serpent so that if they stare at it after being bitten they would be saved... Israel certainly became a mighty nation to be feared & so was feared... So much so Balak King of Moab sent for the prophet Balaam to curse the Israelites not knowing that the El whom Balaam served was YHWH the same El as the Israelites... Balaam did not realise at first who these people were that Balak wanted him to curse until he gave prayer to YHWH... Balak offered Balaam anything he wanted but Balaam refused saying "even for a house full of silver I cannot go beyond the Word of YHWH my El to do less or more"... however Balaam's donkey rebuked him 3 times because he could not see the Angel of YHWH standing before him... The donkey saw & tried to warn him... Both he & the donkey almost met death but YHWH's grace & timeliness saved them...

Day 64: Balaam prophesizes... & YHWH condemns the backsliders...

Numbers 23, 24, 25

Imagine that Balak in his delusion did not understand YHWH was the Creator... He offered Balaam all the gold he could have but Balaam's reverent fear for The Father was greater... He knew YHWH & understood that no perishable thing was better than the eternal things of YHWH... So Israel was truly blessed by Balaam through the words of YHWH & Balak was cursed... Then as has been their pattern Israel's children took up worshipping Baal of Peor the false Moabite god & fornicating with their women... YHWH commanded their destruction but Phinehas grandson of Aaron destroyed an Israelite & his Midianite woman and as such made atonement for Israel... YHWH made an everlasting covenant of peace to him & his descendants for his act of zealous faith...

Day 65: 2nd census but all males perish...

Numbers 26, 27

YHWH commanded a 2nd census of Israelite males over 20 years but none survived the wilderness as YHWH had sentenced... however the daughters of Manasseh were set to lose their inheritance as YHWH's decree to all the tribes born from the Twelve Tribes were traditionally handed to males... YHWH changed the decree so the inheritance could go to daughters if no sons... to siblings if no daughters... & to other close relatives if no siblings... Joshua was then chosen to lead the Exodus as Moses time of demise was nearing... Moses was instructed to inaugurate him before all the Israelites & to set him as the leader of them all... YHWH was very clear of His vision... the disobedience of YHWH's people was no longer tolerated & an annihilation of thousands took place... every man over 20 years old except Caleb & Joshua...

Day 66: List of dedicated offerings...

Numbers 28, 29, 30

Moses was given command by YHWH to instruct His people in the circumspect ways of offering in regards to feasts including: daily, monthly, Sabbath, Passover, Feast of Weeks, Feast of Trumpets, Feast of Tabernacles & Day of Atonement... Hundreds of rams, bulls, lambs & goats were used as well as hundred weights of fine flour, oil & wine... all as offering to YHWH always for atonement of sin... It may not be understood by me why the specific numbers in animals & weight but it is clear from YHWH's Words, in order for forgiveness blood must be shed... In terms of the flour, oil & wine YHWH speaks of all the offerings as "sweet smelling aroma"... Is this literal or metaphorical? Having to prepare these regulated offerings would be a constant reminder of obedience & humility... as humans we are patterned in everything we do & YHWH manifests this in His Ways also...

Day 67: Midianites destroyed... Reuben, Dan & Manasseh stay...

Numbers 31, 32

YHWH commands Moses to destroy Midian because they sinned terribly against Him... even Balaam was slain because he encouraged Midianite women to lay down with the Israelites... 32,000 of them... only Midianite female virgins survived... 12,000 soldiers fought... 1000 from each of the Twelve Tribes & not one lost his life... The awesome power of YHWH cannot be beaten & neither can those He gives this power to... So YHWH permitted on their request that Reuben & Gad can possess the land preventing them crossing the Jordan but only if they make themselves available to fight war & ensure the safe arrival of the Israelites into the Promise Land... YHWH extended this land to half the tribe of Manasseh also...

Day 68: Places travelled through the Exodus...

Numbers 33, 34

The Israelites travelled for over 40 years from the day they left Egypt till they reached Canaan the land of milk & honey that YHWH had promised them... they moved from place to place... camp to camp... saw deaths... victories in war... inaugurations... births... diseases... healing... miracles... prophecies... apostasy... disobedience... & faithfulness... By YHWH's power they reached their Land & it was divided fairly between 9 ½ tribes as Gad, Reuben & half the tribe of Manasseh had their inherited land on the other side of the Jordan... In order for the tribes to possess Canaan & live there in peace they were instructed by YHWH to annihilate the inhabitants as they were an abomination to YHWH... YHWH told them if they didn't the punishment of Canaan would fall on them & that they would reside in irritation & harassment always...

Day 69: Cities of refuge within Levitical cities...

Numbers 35, 36

YHWH commanded that all the tribes donate cities & common land to the Levites from their inheritance... & that 6 cities & a further 42 cities should be put aside as cities of refuge for those who kill accidentally... YHWH set laws for the Levites to regulate this... YHWH also confirmed that the daughters of Zelophedad marry within their tribe to preserve their inheritance... so they married their uncle's sons... They were from the tribe of Manasseh & as their fathers died but were not of those who revolted against YHWH & perished as a result they were given their father's inheritance in place of male heirs as there was none... Everything we need to know YHWH surely makes known to us... however our minds need to be uncontaminated to hear Him clearly & precisely by taking good care of our spiritual, biological, psychological & emotional health...

Day 70: Moses recalls the 40 years' sojourn through the wilderness...

Deuteronomy 1, 2

Moses spoke to the Israelites of all YHWH had spoken to him… He told them to possess the land of the Canaanites & the Amorites the land he swore to their fathers' Abraham, Isaac & Jacob for them & every generation after them… Leaders of each tribe were appointed to assist Moses in judging cases because the Israelites had multiplied numerously "as the stars of Heaven"… He then recalled why a whole generation of male Israelites perished in the wilderness forfeiting entry into the Promised Land… They had refused to fight against the Amorites after the 12 spies returned with discouraging words & fear of their enemies as being "greater & taller"… Only Caleb & Joshua remained as well as Moses… however he too had the promise of entering the land taken away… YHWH never relinquishes on His promises… He promised & gave the land to Esau & to Lot also…

Day 71: Og & Sihon's defeat retold...

Deuteronomy 3, 4

Og King of Bashan & Sihon king of the Amorites were defeated by Israel by the power of YHWH & their land given to all the descendants of Abraham, Isaac & Jacob as promised… Moses reminded them all to keep the commandments through remembering all that YHWH had done… miracles that had never been seen before… It was all so amazing & the zeal Moses had for YHWH was so apparent yet the people still went against YHWH to worship other false gods & go according to their own desires… It seems they were unable to resist feeding their flesh for they wanted things now rather than waiting for YHWH's rewards… it is just the same today… people chasing the things of the world rather than the things of the Spirit… Father may I never leave You lest I die…

Day 72: Moses continues recalling YHWH's commands...

Deuteronomy 5, 6, 7

Moses reminded the people of YHWH's commandments & how they feared being destroyed because they could hear His Voice... YHWH shared His desire for them to always have a reverent fear for Him... YHWH shares His love for His people not because they are mighty but because He made a promise to their forefathers for thousands of generations to come... & that it should be a constant reminder to them forever... Disobedience shall be dealt with severely with no mercy... The Israelites are YHWH's chosen people... He dispossessed lands of apostates & gave to His chosen even though initially these idolaters were greater... Canaanites, Hivites, Amorites, Perrizzites, Jebusites, Gergashites & Hittites... they were all utterly destroyed... YHWH promised continued blessings in every aspect of their life as a reward for obedience...

Day 73: YHWH's love despite disobedience...

Deuteronomy 8, 9, 10

Despite the Israelites constant moaning & disrespect of YHWH's blessings & commandments He still gave the promise land for them to possess... not for their righteousness because they weren't... they were hard of hearing & stubborn... but because of the wickedness of those who were already dwelling in the land & because He made the promise to their forefathers Abraham, Isaac & Jacob... What a loving Father he is & how painful it must be for Him when we go away from all He is & all He gives us to go to serve the enemy... Yes it states He is a jealous El but unless we put all our faith in Him we cannot adopt the mind of Him... that then leaves our minds open to being manipulated by Satan whose ultimate aim is to steal, kill & destroy through machinations & deception... May I always have total faith in You Father & Your Promise to me...

Day 74: Love YHWH your El lest you suffer...

Deuteronomy 11, 12, 13

Moses instructed the people again to remember all that YHWH had done for them since their deliverance from Egypt... YHWH promised them a land luscious, fruitful & bountiful... blessed with rain from Heaven in its season from early rain to latter rain... but should they disobey Him & go to serve any other gods then no rain shall fall, the land will yield nothing & they will perish... YHWH prepared them for the cross over to Jordan into the promise land along with how & where they should worship... & with instructions on destroying utterly the false gods, the images & pillars... burning everything... YHWH was very specific on them following His laws & that any who attempted to corrupt them with false doctrines should be stoned to death...

Day 75: Feasts revisited...

Deuteronomy 14, 15, 16

Moses reminds the Israelites of their duties towards the sacred feasts to YHWH... he reminds them that they are a Holy people to YHWH and as such must give their tithes, feed the poor & needy, release debt and servants in the 7th year and serve their El YHWH faithfully... do all this and YHWH will surely bless you for eternity... May I be continually part of Your Community Father that I may do good in Your eyes, give Your Love to others, adhere to Your Words, exemplify you & be an ambassador for You so that all who witness Your Light in me will want to know You & serve You also... Amen!

Day 76: Do not serve other gods or mediums…

Deuteronomy 17, 18, 19, 20

Moses continues to instruct the Israelites of YHWH's laws… he prophesies that a Saviour is to come carrying the Word of YHWH… that all must listen to this One lest they have to give back their life… YHWH finds all clairvoyance, witchcraft, sorcery & soothsaying an abomination… He instructs appointed kings to copy the Book of the Law & read daily to uphold all that is righteous & holy & good… YHWH never lets His people down… He protects them always in their obedience & loyalty to Him…

Day 77: YHWH's laws continue...

Deuteronomy 21, 22, 23

Moses continues to recall all the laws YHWH has set for adherence by His people... there were laws concerning all things from unsolved murders to illegitimate births... from 1st born rights to rights of virginity... YHWH is aware of all those thoughts, words & deeds that are not righteous... that are signs of deceit & evil and therefore put measures in place to eradicate them before it becomes a 'disease' to the spirit... It really is that we must trust Him... He knows best... He is The Creator of all after all...

Day 78: Blessings or curses...

Deuteronomy 28, 29

Wow to those who are obedient to all of YHWH's laws... & woe to those who are not... YHWH promises an abundance of life to all those faithful & loyal to Him... blessings of marriage, children, livestock, grain, fruit, health, rain, leadership & protection... But oh, the treacherous curses to those who are disobedient & put other false gods before YHWH... an astonishment to the world, a disease, a worthless race left to the scavengers of the earth, pitied & ridiculed... I know what I would choose & not just to receive the blessings... but because I know He is & will always be The Almighty, The Creator of all things, The One True El... loved & revered by His Loyal Ones...

Day 79: All the Laws finally spoken...

Deuteronomy 30, 31

So all the Laws, commandments, statues & judgments were spoken fully by Moses through YHWH's instruction... the entire congregation were given the choice of life & good or death & evil... Moses finished writing the Laws in the Book & was instructed to place it in The Ark which the Levites were to take care of... YHWH instructed Moses to write a song so the Law can be remembered... Joshua was inaugurated as leader as Moses was not to enter the Promise Land... He was 120 years old when YHWH told him his death was imminent... Even though the choice of life & death was given, that YHWH had spoken the wonderful blessings of following Him & the devastating curses if they didn't... He knew that the people would still turn aside from His Laws even before they entered the Land flowing of milk & honey... How deeply fallible, weak, disloyal & greedy man is...

Day 80: Moses dies...

Deuteronomy 32, 33, 34; Psalms 91

Moses was the mightiest of all the prophets... he was given an enormous task to lead the Israelites out of Egypt & he did... by the Almighty strength of YHWH... with wisdom... knowledge... endurance... love... & long-suffering... Despite all that YHWH did through Moses the Israelites still sinned & turned against Him... Moses believed he was an Egyptian but learning his true identity he waited with integrity to know YHWH & when he did he dedicated himself fully to the work YHWH set before him... Unfortunately he did not enter the earthly Promise Land because the sins of the people anger him & caused him to lose sight of YHWH's holiness... never-the-less Moses died on Mount Nebo having received the promise of eternity with YHWH... YHWH gives this promise to all His creations... to those who keep His commands... who love YHWH with all their strength, soul, & mind... loving their neighbour & themselves in the same way... A life not serving YHWH is truly a life in hell with no peace for the soul...

Day 81: Joshua leads...

Joshua 1, 2, 3, 4

Joshua is now YHWH's great prophet after the death of Moses... YHWH instructs Joshua to prepare the people to go over the Jordan into the Promised Land... Joshua sends spies to Jericho... they are hidden by a harlot called Rahab who asks in return for her & her family to be favoured by YHWH... it is evident her faith saves her & her kin... Joshua then chooses a leader from each of the Twelve Tribes to lead their tribe after the Levites have gone forth with The Ark... As the Levites feet have all been immersed into the River Jordan YHWH stopped up the flow of the river so all of Israel could cross on dry ground... 12 stones representing each tribe was laid on the dry ground of the Jordan before YHWH released the waters after every Israelite had crossed over... Then each of the stones that each of the Twelve Tribe leader's picked from within the Jordan was assembled as a memorial for all time to commemorate the crossing through the Jordan River on dry ground... Joshua had truly received the power of YHWH that all of Israel were witness to...

Day 82: Jericho & Ai dispossessed for Israel…

Joshua 5, 6, 7, 8

So the 40 years of wandering through the Wilderness was over & the Israelites no longer had to eat the manna… had they not continued sinning their time in the Wilderness would've been shorter… a whole generation had to perish and the Promised Land was taken away by YHWH… however He continued to bless them with fertile land & produce… The walls of Jericho came down & Ai was emptied & set on fire so that Israel could have the cities that YHWH promised… Blessings for obedience… curses for disobedience as Achan from the family of Judah experienced… him & all his household perished because he hid accursed spoil from their destruction of Jericho… a stone mound that covered their corpses remains outside the city to this day…

Day 83: Wars won... Promised Land won...

Joshua 9, 10, 11

Joshua led Israel in many battles instructed by YHWH... & all of them were won... YHWH fought with them even destroying the wicked with hailstones... only the Hivites survived because of the fear of Israel when they tricked Joshua into believing they were from afar when they were really from local... Their lives were spared as a result & to this day their role in Israel are as woodcutters & water carriers... Joshua & Israel were indeed mighty & the world feared them... The land YHWH had promised them was won & they finally rested from war... thank YHWH!

Day 84: Judah & Caleb blessed with land...

Joshua 12, 13, 14, 15

Moses & Joshua conquered between them 33 kings & as a result rested from war & secured luscious & fertile land as an inheritance for all the Twelve Tribes except the Levites whose inheritance is YHWH... Caleb was given a special inheritance as the only male survivor along with Joshua from his generation... he remained obedient to YHWH & an encouragement to his people... YHWH kept His promise but there was still more land for them to claim... however YHWH gave them rest... for now...

Day 85: Manasseh, Ephraim & Benjamin's inheritance...

Joshua 16, 17, 18

So the children of Joseph, Manasseh & Ephraim, were given their lot as divided by Joshua & Moses remembering that the Tribe of Manasseh was halved & given separate inheritance on either side of the Jordan... The Manasseh Tribe grew large & requested more land that Joshua as a servant of YHWH gave them... Benjamin's land was also apportioned... 26 cities in all including Jerusalem... Where are the True Israelites now? YHWH spoke that He would give their inheritance to a stupid race due to their disobedience... Is this what has happened that they no longer lay claim to any land? Muslims & Arabs have inheritance in these places but I have no knowledge of any of the Twelve Tribes having a stake...

Day 86: All YHWH's Words came to pass…

Joshua 19, 20, 21

So said… so done… The Promise YHWH made to Abraham, Isaac & Jacob finally came to pass & every family of the Twelve Tribes was apportioned their Land… The Levites had no land as an inheritance but were apportioned cities from the other tribes to dwell in… Joshua was given his own city as a reward… YHWH finally gave them rest from war & rest in the total fulfilment of His Words… Amen!

Day 87: Covenant in Shechem...

Joshua 22, 23, 24

And so Joshua died but not before making a covenant with Israel to serve YHWH alone... that YHWH's blessings have all stood but the curses will also for those who sin against YHWH & serve other gods... Phinehas died also & both were buried on the land which they inherited... The Reubenites, Gadites & half tribe of Manasseh were given the blessing to return to the land they chose on either side of the Jordan... Gilead... They were so thankful to YHWH they built an altar as a witness on the Jordan... but the other tribes of Israel thought it was an altar to foreign gods & threatened war against them... They were wrong & learnt this after Phinehas went to speak to them along with leaders from each tribe... The Twelve Tribes were now settled & made a promise to continue serving YHWH... these all witnessed directly the power & miracles of The Almighty Father...

Day 88: Conquered remains with the conqueror...

Judges 1, 2

All the tribes fought and won the land YHWH had promised them but were not able to overcome all of the original inhabitants... so those that remained lived amongst them in tribute... Long after Joshua died and all those from his generation, the next generation of Israelites transgressed and started to worship Baals... So the curse YHWH made was upon them and He delivered Israel up to their enemies.... Even when He appointed Judges the people still disobeyed them and through their disobedience they suffered distress at the hands of their enemies as they had forsaken YHWH...

Day 89: Judges & YHWH's mighty men...

Judges 3, 4, 5

Othniel, Shamgar, Ehud & Balak... these were men that YHWH raised up to deliver Israel after they had suffered at the hands of the enemy because they had sinned against YHWH by serving the foreign gods... As a generation was delivered then died, the new generation that did not know of YHWH or His Miracles would go back to worshipping the Baals & again YHWH would give them up to their enemies... but their cry for deliverance would never fall on deaf ears & The Father YHWH would always hear them & raise up a deliverer to save them... YHWH also appointed Judges to hear cases & cast judgement.... This is the first time I've known a woman to be appointed... Deborah... She won victory over Sisera when she went out to war against him & his thousands on the request of Balak... A song was sung in her honour & that of Jael the Kenite... Another woman of YHWH tricked Sisera into believing she would hide him from Israel... She gave him milk & drove a peg through his temple with a hammer... Israel experienced decades of rest but equally decades of captivity...

Day 90: YHWH raises Gideon…

Judges 6, 7

As was the regular occurrence of disobedience of Israel they were now in the hands of the Midianites… & as was the undeserved kindness of YHWH after hearing their cries He raised up a prophet called Gideon who considered himself small & lacking amongst his brethren… His father renamed him Jerubbaal after he destroyed the altars of Baal & his brethren wanted to kill him… His father said… "Let Baal contend against him"… So YHWH sent Gideon & a chosen 300 men to fight the Midianites who were as numerous as the sand grains… yet Gideon won… But Gideon tested the spirit a few times… with sacrifices, with signs on the threshing floor & with foretelling of dreams… The Princes of Midian Oreb & Zeeb were killed at the rock & wine press of their namesake respectively… YHWH as always prevailed & delivered Israel yet again… How faithful, loving & almighty our Father YHWH is…

Day 91: Gideon refuses Kingship...

Judges 8, 9

Gideon saved his people from oppression for several decades but when he died Israel sinned by following foreign gods again... He was approached to serve as king by his people but he told them... "YHWH is your king"... After his death Abimelech his son for a slave persuaded the people to have him as king rather than Gideon's 70 sons... they accepted and he and his callous men killed all Gideon's sons bar one... Jotham... He gathered the people of Shechem and encouraged them to go against Abimelech... YHWH avenged the blood of Gideon's 70 sons and Abimelech was killed by a stone falling on his head by a woman... Unwilling to be remembered by this he asked one of his men to thrust a sword through him so as to account this as the cause of his death... even at death his pride was ahead of him...

Day 92: **Samson the Nazarite...**

Judges **13, 14, 15**

Samson was a special judge raised up by YHWH... His mother was barren when an Angel of YHWH came to tell her she will bear a son & no grape or unclean food should pass through her during her pregnancy for her son shall be raised a Nazarite... Samson was exceptionally gifted with physical strength... He desired a Timnite woman as his wife against his parents wish but unbeknown to them it was the works of YHWH... He loved his wife but she betrayed him... her father betrayed him & his own people betrayed him also because of the Philistines might & oppression... He was angry but continued to experience a physical strength like no others... The Spirit of YHWH was truly with him...

Day 93: Samson perishes... Israel is judgeless...

Judges 16, 17, 18

Samson's weakness was women... & a woman was his ultimate downfall... he gave away the secret of his strength to the harlot Delilah and as a result was captured & blinded by the Philistines... They gave sacrifice & worship to their god Dagon for delivering Samson into their hands... little did they think that his hair would grow back & so his strength would also return... Faithful to YHWH he prayed for the strength to destroy the Philistines for blinding him... YHWH again was with him... Samson died along with the 3000+ Philistines & his corpse was taken away by his brothers and buried with Manoah his father...

Day 94: Benjamites commit murder & perish...

Judges 19, 20, 21

No king or judge was ruling in these days & the people were committing all manner of sin... debauchery... rape... murder... A Levite with his concubine passing through Gibeah the land of the Benjamites was kindly taken in by an old man to spend a night safely before continuing their travel to their home in the mountains of Ephraim... Disgusting men of the Benjamites came to the old man at night demanding sex with the Levite... Outraged the old man offered his daughter & concubine instead... They took the concubine & raped her all night till she died... The Levite rode home cut her into 12 pieces & distributed her amongst the Twelve Tribes... Israel waged war against the Benjamites with YHWH's permission & 25,000 of them perished... however 600 fled & hid in the rock of Rimmon for 4 months... Israel grieved for their lost tribe... however the 600 men were given another chance... Israel instructed them to go down to Shiloh & whilst the women there dancing as part of the wine festival to take for themselves a wife... So said so done... The evil & treachery that happens when man turns away from YHWH or does not heed the Creators ways... Sin befalls all but when you are not with YHWH you have no chance of overpowering or overcoming it and instead it will consume you to death...

Day 95: Faithful Ruth...

Ruth 1, 2, 3, 4

Beautiful story of Ruth who never forsook her mother-in-law Naomi who lost her husband too & both sons... As a Moabite she left her family & religion to follow that of Naomi's... She made an everlasting claim that YHWH will be her El & His people shall be her people... so said so done... Ruth was remarried to Boaz from the line of Judah... They bore a son Obed & became the great-grandparents of David King of Israel... YHWH surely blessed Ruth for her faithfulness, mercy & love!

Day 96: Samuel... Hannah's gift to YHWH

1 Samuel 1, 2, 3

Hannah was the favourite of Elkanah's two wives but was barren... this grieved her so especially as Peninnah, the other wife would taunt her because she did have children... Elkanah wondered why Hannah grieved... but I understand... she's a woman who felt unfulfilled... Hannah's faith allowed her to petition to YHWH & He heard her prayer... She gave birth to the prophet Samuel & as promised she gave him to minister for YHWH when he was weaned... YHWH surely gifted her... she honoured her promise to Him & He gave her three more sons & two daughters... She trusted the FATHER... Meanwhile YHWH put a curse on the house of Eli due to the sinful behaviour of his two sons Phinehas & Hophni... The prophesy was given to Samuel for Eli... Both his sons would die within 24 hours & no man would grow old in the house of Eli forever... They profaned the priestly sacrifice & fornicated... In the sight of YHWH they were detestable... but Samuel was obedient & highly favoured...

Day 97: White-washed stones of YHWH's Laws...

Deuteronomy 24, 25, 26, 27

Moses almost comes to an end with recalling the Laws of YHWH to the Israelites as they are about to enter the Promised Land... They are instructed to white wash the large stones with lime and to write all the laws on them that were instructed through Moses by YHWH... These were the laws that governed righteous behaviour & rituals of worship... The rituals had to be performed regularly to atone for sin... Now thank YHWH our exercising of faith in Yahsah our Messiah is the ultimate atonement...

Day 98: More judges to fight & rule for Israel...

Judges 10, 11, 12

YHWH was dejected when once again Israel sinned against him to worship other gods... He denied their plea for deliverance but retracted when they made a promise to return to Him & serve other gods no more... YHWH continued to raise up judges, mighty men to fight & rule over them... Israel was indeed a mighty race with everything they needed if they remained faithful to YHWH... but time & time again once a judge died they would forget the blessings of YHWH & sin... so Israel brought judgement & punishment upon themselves... YHWH reminded the Gentiles that their lack of cooperation led them to lose their land to be repossessed by Israel...

Day 99: Philistines steal The Ark...

1 Samuel 4, 5, 6, 7, 8

Samuel continued to judge & serve as prophet for Israel all the days of his life... Israel continued to sin & every battle bar one was lost by them to the Philistines... Eli's sons both died in the war... & Eli died when the news was brought to him... he fell backwards & broke his neck... The Ark was stolen by The Philistines... they paid a heavy price for stealing it... tumours, diseases & death befell them... They placed the Ark by the idol of Dagon their god... Dagon was found later on the ground beheaded & hands cut off... After 7 months they made golden sacrifices and put the Ark on a new cart pulled by cows never yoked and sent it back to Beth Shemesh in Israel... 50,000 Israelites perished by YHWH for looking into the Ark... The Israelites were truly a disobedient people... Samuel set up his two sons Joel & Abiyah to judge in his old age but even they committed sinful acts... so the people requested a king to rule after Samuel which offended Samuel... however YHWH said to Samuel they have not rejected you but rejected Me... give them what they request but let them know the king they will have will oppress & enslave them... Despite this knowledge they still wanted a king...

Day 100: Saul crowned the King of Israel...

1 Samuel 9, 10, 11, 12

Saul was a Benjamite the son of Kish... He was considered the most handsome of Israel & the tallest... He stood out amongst all his brethren... He was astounded when he was told by the prophet Samuel that he will be king... He considered himself least of the Benjamites & the Benjamites least of all the Twelve Tribes... "Is Saul also amongst the prophets" became a famous saying because YHWH had changed his heart & he began prophesying with the other known prophets... However YHWH gave a message to Samuel for the people... because they had asked for a king from YHWH He gave them one... but good between them & their king will come only if they are obedient to His Ways... but if they turned aside from Him then His Hand will be against them & their king... Knowing the Israelites from reading previous written chapters it was inevitable that they would sin again... It appears the nature of the flesh... but evident of YHWH's Words all those obedient to Him will reap blessings & all those disobedient to Him will reap curses... Faith is the key... so too the knowledge of YHWH's love & wisdom... The Scriptures is evidence of YHWH & to heed His Word is the most profitable thing we can do as His creations...

Day 101: Saul & Jonathan win wars...

1 Samuel 13, 14

Saul was 30 when he was crowned king over Israel & he reigned 42 years... He fought many wars with his son Jonathan & his 1st cousin Abner the commander of his army... YHWH was with them & gave the Amalekites, Edomites, Moabites & Philistines into his hand... Saul had made a vow that no man shall eat until vengeance was taken on his enemy but Jonathan didn't hear & ate the honey in the forest... he was condemned to die but the people made petition to YHWH because he had fought well for them & as a result their petition saved him... Are these physical wars or spiritual wars... or both? So much warring & fighting... It makes you wonder that if Israel were loyal & faithful would there be any fighting? Certainly the warring would occur between the flesh & the Spirit but faith in YHWH would allow the Spirit to always win... Amen!

Day 102: David anointed king over Saul...

1 Samuel 15, 16, 17

King Saul disobeyed The Father as it was spoken by Samuel... "Obedience is better than sacrifice"... Saul had kept the plunder & the king of the Amalekites even though YHWH commanded him to destroy it all... From then YHWH commanded Samuel to anoint another as king... David the youngest of Jesse's eight sons... ruddy & good-looking... He became the soothing musician to Saul when the spirit of distress was upon him... YHWH also gave him power to take down the Philistine giant Goliath... David truly walked in faith & in total loyalty to YHWH... he let Goliath know that because of his arrogance, audacity & defiance YHWH will deliver him into his hand for destruction... so said so done... not with a sword but a sling shot to his head... with a sword David beheaded his corpse... Saul was in awe of him & asked... "Whose son are you?" David had amazed everyone...

Day 103: Saul's wickedness toward David...

1 Samuel 18, 19, 20; Psalms 11, 59

David as humble as he was shone bright & beautiful by the Power of YHWH... The people sang a song giving him praise over 10,000 & Saul praises over 1,000... Saul resented this & believed that all that was left was for David to be crowned King... so from then his envy turned the desire of his heart to machinate wickedness against David... had YHWH not provided the love & loyalty of Jonathan & his wife Michal (Saul's children) David would have perished... Envy leads to confusion & all kinds of evil... the disobedience of heart is akin to the envy of spirit & both bring forth desires of the heart that give birth to sin... The very flesh of us is sinful by nature no matter how much we want to believe it isn't... Our only recourse is to follow with diligence the Way of Yahsah the Messiah... He desired nothing fleshly but only to do YHWH's will... for us to love YHWH completely & love our neighbours the same... this takes absolute humility... letting go of self & our fleshly desires wanting only the things that please YHWH... to use the gifts YHWH has given us to shine His light that it may engender salvation for all who are witnesses... Seek to find your gifts through pray... meditation... the daily reading of Scriptures... & fasting... all thru the guidance of YHWH's Spirit...

Day 104: David's mercy upon Saul...

1 Samuel 21, 22, 23, 24

Oh how the envy & fleshly desires of the heart eventually consumes the mind & turns it into abhorrent wickedness... Saul's thoughts were obsessed with annihilating David that all reason had left him... He killed the priest Abimelech who did nothing but show hospitality to David knowing nothing about Saul's mission to kill him... Sheer wickedness was in Saul's heart yet when David was given the opportunity to kill Saul love & mercy were in his heart & so he spared him... Saul was overwhelmed with shame, guilt & repentance... He knew David had all the qualities of a righteous king & as well as blessing him in his future kingship he requested David spare his life & that of his progeny... David was very special & highly favoured in the Eyes of YHWH... & these acts of mercy evidences why...

Day 105: YHWH's protection & comfort...

Psalms 7, 27, 31, 34, 52

Oh how ultimately beautiful it is to know the True El YHWH & His Son Yahsah our Messiah... having full assurance of every Word that is YHWH's... Until the Holy Spirit dwells in us we can never have full access to the accurate knowledge of Truth... YHWH makes us specific promises... to His righteous... & to the wicked... David is prime example of the struggles, condemnation & tribulation true righteous people experience... He was humble in his ways, merciful, loving & faithful... yet Saul sought to kill him primarily because YHWH had given him natural gifts... This is exactly how it is today... that YHWH's blessings on His children are envied by those who do not receive theirs because their heart is not clean... they are not in the Word daily but listen to the doctrines of men...

Day 106: **David's faith abounds...**

Psalms **56, 120, 140, 141, 142**

David truly knew YHWH... & put totally trust in Him... I can fully resonate with David because of my own tribulations & persecutions... For me it is no longer about hoping in YHWH... it is purely about knowing for sure He is real... feeling His love & knowing without a doubt He exist... I know that all the adversities I have gone through have allowed me to grow in faith... it couldn't have happened otherwise... The Scripture in JAMES (1:2-4) now has new revised meaning to me... "Count it all joy when you fall upon various trials... knowing the testing of your faith leads to endurance... but let endurance have its complete work that you may be perfect and complete... lacking nothing"... Really you have to experience this transformation in order to understand it... & therefore understand fully David's plight...

Day 107: David marries Abigail & spares Saul again...

1 Samuel 25, 26, 27

David was a warrior seeking refuge in the wilderness because of Saul's envy towards him... He depended on the kindness & mercy of others... This was not given by Nabal a Carmelite business man who was mean & evil... he had a beautiful, understanding wife Abigail... Nabal refused to feed David's men even though David sent words of peace to him & had previously taken care of his servants... Abigail in her righteous wisdom saved David from killing her husband giving him both wise words & provisions... David blessed her & when YHWH destroyed Nabal David took Abigail's hand in marriage... After this again David spared Saul's life... & again Saul sent David away in blessings... It seems obvious that David understood the power of the enemy over the mind of Saul... David knew that Saul was also an anointed of YHWH so his obedience remained... however he continued to live as a refugee at the mercy & kindness of others... & with the total protection of YHWH...

Day 108: David glorifies YHWH…

Psalms 17, 35, 54, 63

David wrote the Psalms inspired by Holy Spirit… He was spiritually afflicted all his life & his recounting in Psalms is an example for us… I resonate & empathise with David… as YHWH's children we are a royal priesthood… a peculiar race… & the world will always fight against us… What is more astonishing is those that say they are on the side of YHWH fight against us also just as in David's days… He knew the Father & as such knew he had full blessings of the FATHER… his praises, glory, prayers & blessings were from the depths of his heart… faithful & true… He loved the Father explicitly & absolutely… He had such a love for those who were YHWH's… He truly exemplifies our way & mirrors our experiences… almost like Yahsah… the difference however David was a man… flawed… unlike Yahsah who was, is & will always be… PERFECT…

Day 109: David's blessings...Saul's destruction...

1 Samuel 28, 29, 30, 31; Psalms 18

David had YHWH on his side always... terribly afflicted David's faith in YHWH never failed... However Saul continued to go against YHWH visiting a medium & asking for Samuel to be raised from the dead... Samuel came up but gave him devastating news of his demise as well as his sons'... So said so done... he & his sons were killed in battle & Saul's corpse was disrespectfully put on display... As YHWH had revealed to him his downfall so it took place... He had been given a great honour & opportunity by the Father but his ego & arrogance allowed his judgement to be corrupted by the enemy... why revel in your own glory for a short while when YHWH promises glory in Him for eternity? Because the enemy makes people believe the money & materialism of this life along with their own importance is everything... when in fact it is nothing & means nothing in the end...

Day 110: The comfort of Psalms...

Psalms 121, 123, 124, 125, 128, 129, 130

Psalms are a gift of David inspired by Holy Spirit... absolutely everything we experience in our spiritual life (which indubitably connects to all aspects of our life) can be seen in the Psalms & therefore gives us peace, mercy and reassurance... One of my favourite verses "If YHWH should watch our errors who could stand? There is true forgiveness with Him in order that He may be feared" (130:3,4)... Such a powerful scripture... In truly experiencing His Forgiveness You know that He is real & alive... & in knowing that He is real you then come to a realisation that everything He promises He will deliver... all the blessings & reassurances He gives in the Word will ALL come to pass... wow... Therefore for all of us who obey His Word... who walk in the Light that is His Son... who love Him & our neighbours (for love covers a multitude of sins)... the promise of eternal life living as royalty with our precious Fathers is ours... Amen!

Day 111: David mourns Saul & Jonathan...

2 Samuel 1, 2, 3, 4

David was full of grief when he was given the news of Jonathan & Saul's death... he mourned greatly for them & killed the man who brought the news for he had finished Saul's life, an anointed of YHWH (even though it was at Saul's request)... David became King of Judah & Ishbosheth Saul's son became King of Israel... However Baanah & Rechab, Isbosheth's captains killed him in his bed & brought his head to David... David killed them for their wicked act against a righteous one... he also put a curse on the house of Joab & Abishai for killing Saul's captain Abner, who had made peace with David & planned to give him Israel as a kingdom... So much warring & killing... wickedness & righteousness continually fought & still do today... Thank YHWH that the fight is fought and won by Him & His Son & that all we have to do is remain faithful & obedient... believing without doubt that all things are well with Him...

Day 112: Psalms... Words of Protection...

Psalms 6, 8, 9, 10, 14, 16, 19, 21

"And those who know Your name will put their trust in You… for You YHWH have not forsaken those who seek You"… It is a tragedy that the wicked do not accept that YHWH is the Most High & go about causing grief for the righteous… For transient pleasures they relinquish eternal joy… Through envy for the temporary things of life they take the life of those who love YHWH… then lose theirs forever… I will remain forever with You my Father & sit next to Your Son my Messiah Yahsah… only with Your strength, mercy & love…

Day 113: Descendants of Adam...

1 Chronicles 1, 2

Chronicles list the genealogy of YHWH's people & those who turned away... Joab, who killed Abner, was David's nephew, his sister Zeruiah's child... In other words David had his nephew killed for his wickedness... I suppose that blood & spirit means the same... If we commit evil against YHWH, being a blood relative or not means nothing... The righteous can plead on behalf of the wrong-doer dependent on the wrong-doings...

Day 114: Peace in Psalms...

Psalms 43, 44, 45, 49, 84, 85, 87

The Psalms are incredible... they surely chronicle the journey of David but also all those who are walking & witnessing their life in YHWH... There is a lot to digest & understand but thank YHWH we have help from His Holy Spirit...

Day 115: Judah heads the Twelve Tribes...

1 Chronicles 3, 4, 5

David had nineteen sons but that did not include sons he had with his concubines... Reuben, Jacob's eldest, lost his birth right because he took his father's concubine... Judah then became head of the Twelve Tribes & from him came Yahsah the Ruler (in the flesh) due to Joseph's birth right... Reuben, Gad & the half tribe of Manasseh turned to worship false gods & to this day lost their inheritance...

Day 116: Israel forgot YHWH & suffered...

Psalms 73, 77, 78

How many times did Israel sin against YHWH despite all His blessings, mercies & miracles? & how many times did He forgive them despite their selfish, unfaithful ways? Too many to count... How hurtful & painful... The Tribes missed out on their glory & Judah was given the ultimate blessing... David was chosen as His servant over all... this meek, young shepherd who loved YHWH with all his heart... who was persecuted for no other reason than he was blessed by YHWH... YHWH forgave His people because their flesh made them weak... how loving and merciful He is...

Day 117: The Levites...

1 Chronicles 6

The Levites are set aside to minister especially & specifically to YHWH... Aaron & his sons were given the duties of the Most Holy to perform before YHWH... that was the Levites inheritance... They owned no land but each of the three families of the sons of Levi, Kothathites, Merarites & Gershonites, were given habitat from their brothers of the rest of The 12 Tribes...

Day 118: Glory of YHWH...

Psalms 81, 88, 92, 93

Oh how blessed we are... those who truly wait upon YHWH... Everything YHWH promises is ours... He is everlasting... He is loving-kindness itself... He has made it clear that when we disobey & sin against him pain & suffering befalls us... David suffered mental torment because of Saul's envy but not because of his own sin... Satan attacks our minds but YHWH promises redemption... It is our true faith in Him that allows us to believe this... & when we truly believe we are delivered... Amen!

Day 119: Genealogy of the Twelve Tribes...

1 Chronicles 7, 8, 9, 10

1 Chronicles continues to chronicle the generations of the Twelve Tribes... It states Judah taken captive by Babylon & the duties of the Levites in Jerusalem... The death of Saul & his sons is repeated only this time Saul falls on his sword unaided so here we have a different recounting from the story told in 1 Samuel... Saul lost his life for his unfaithfulness & for consulting a medium...

Day 120: Mercies forever...

Psalms 102, 103, 104

David has a total grasp of the righteous man's plight... He is so eloquent & articulate in his retrospection that he totally enables spiritual understanding of the inner conflicts... YHWH supplies everything we need & fully understands we are in the flesh therefore susceptible to the temptations of the flesh... it is almost an inevitability... However our goal is to manage the flesh by feeding the Spirit with the Word of YHWH & living practically & psychologically by the Word through administration... To say we do not sin or never sin renders us & YHWH liars... it's impossible not to in our flesh otherwise what would be the point of Yahsah's ultimate sacrifice... It's the practice of sin that abhors the Father... knowingly continuing to sin in apathy or arrogance... While the Spirit is fed & grows as a by-product the flesh deteriorates & withers...

Day 121: King David & his great army...

2 Samuel 5; 1 Chronicles 11, 12

David reigned as King of Judah & Israel for a combination of 40 years... He had truly loyal leaders from all the Twelve Tribes approximately 400,000 warriors... Some had left the camp of Saul to support King David... He emulated love & peace & through this won their hearts... The Spirit of YHWH was with him & all those who supported him...

Day 122: To dwell in unity...

Psalms 133

I read this chapter many times for in depth & further understanding… precious oil represents a blessing & when it's poured on your head then that blessing is personal… However running on the beard of Aaron I presume indicated his acceptance as high priest of the sacrifice that cleanses sin on behalf of the Israelites… but now our One & Only High Priest is Yahsah the Messiah… & all we need to do is follow His Way…

Day 123: YHWH's loving-kindness & mercies...

Psalms 106, 107

To imagine how YHWH feels when men go against Him with their wickedness, sins & iniquitous ways is simple... Imagine as a father or mother you constantly take care of your children... feed them, clothe them, protect them, give them fertile land & flock, blessings in abundance, show them kindness, love, mercy, give them wisdom, knowledge & a future of eternal existence in richness & glory... but rather than thanking you, being obedient & following your ways they decide to follow someone else's parents who also feeds them, clothes them, protects in a fleshly sense but lies, cheats, disrespects you the true parent by condemnation & insults... then forgets all the wonderful things you had done for them & that you still would if they returned... You would feel hurt, empty, disheartened, dejected, sad, disappointed, angry... yes this is how our Father YHWH feels towards all those who choose not to accept His Ways... He is the Most High... Creator of this universe & the Only One who can promise eternal existence in Paradise... with Him, His Son, His Angels & all the other righteous ones who wait on Him & exercise faith in His Son Yahsah the Messiah...

Day 124: David brings the Ark back...

1 Chronicles 13, 14, 15, 16

In his quest to bring the Ark back David expressed anger to YHWH because He destroyed a man for touching the Ark... David in retrospect realised that YHWH should have been consulted first... So David gave the Levites charge of taking care of the ark in its return... David was so happy once the Ark came back to Jerusalem that he threw a celebration... he gave every single person bread, meat & a raisin cake... There was music, singing & dance... David dressed especially for the occasion & composed a Psalm especially giving praise to YHWH instructing the people to give praise & expressing how all nature is giving praise including the trees, the mountains & the seas... His wife Michal looked on at his joy with contempt unaware to David... David truly had a deep love in his heart for his Father YHWH... He recognised YHWH had truly blessed him as King of Israel & so did every nation...YHWH had made them fear David & gave all his enemies into his hand... David expressed his gratitude & praise openly & gladly...

Day 125: YHWH gives strength to His people...

Psalms 1, 2, 15, 22, 23, 24, 47, 68

YHWH indeed blesses those who do not walk in the counsel of the ungodly, or do not stand in the path of sinners nor do not sit in the seat of scoffers... but who walk uprightly, speak the truth in their heart & meditate on His Words day & night... We serve an Awesome El, Merciful & True... There for us when we need Him as long as we are not worshipping false idols or speaking deceitfully... He makes us lie in green pastures, restores our soul, prepares a table for us in the midst of enemies... He is there comforting us in the shadow of death... who could ever be mightier than Him? No one... no not one!!!

Day 126: Praise YHWH...

Psalms 89, 96, 100, 101, 105, 132

YHWH is truly merciful, great, awesome, almighty, the One & Only... He swore His Truth & never failed... He is worthy to be praised always & forever... He heals... He anoints... He blesses... He delivers... Psalms is a true depiction of David's experiences... the joy & persecutions... but how through it all he never failed in keeping his faith & love for YHWH...

Day 127: YHWH... His Chosen People... & David...

2 Samuel 6, 7; 1 Chronicles 17

David returned the Ark to his land & he danced in celebration with no ego but humility & innocence... But his wife Michal was resentful saying he was making a fool of himself in front of the Israelite maidens... David unashamedly said these same women will honour me & before my El YHWH I will give praise & worship... & she was barren all the days of her life as a punishment... So David desperately wanted to build a house of cedar for YHWH but the prophet Nathan received word from YHWH that his seed shall build the house (not him)... and that his house will be blessed forever... This pleased David...

Day 128: David continues his conquests...

2 Samuel 8, 9; 1 Chronicles 18

David was a mighty warrior blessed by YHWH... no harm came to him & he was able to subdue hundreds of thousands of his enemies... He always gave worship & sacrifices to YHWH... & showed empathy, love & generosity to those around him... Saul persecuted David to dark & desperate despair but David still maintained humility & kindness towards Saul's family... Jonathan, Saul's son loved David & David returned the love by giving Jonathan's disabled son a place at his table... A true honour & an example of forgiveness & mercy... David put his whole life in YHWH's Hands... Throughout all that he experienced he consulted with YHWH...

Day 129: The Wisdom & Glory of Psalms...

Psalms 25, 29, 33, 36, 39

Everything we need to know as Children of YHWH is written in Psalms... King David was a Child of YHWH... Chronicles states he was the 1st born meaning YHWH had raised him as the 1st anointed of Judah... From his line came Joseph, Yahsah's earthly father... David is a great example of a righteous man even though he sinned YHWH still found favour in him... David experienced tribulation, persecution as well as an abundance of blessings & joy... He recognised his frailty & flaws as a human & understood the almighty creative & protective power of YHWH... He knew that YHWH was the True El... the One & Only El & no other mighty one could compare... He also knew that the righteous would live for eternity with YHWH but that the wicked would perish... He knew that he had to be in prayer with YHWH daily for mercy & guidance... Remaining faithful & true to YHWH means living every day reaching to Him for His Wisdom, His Love & forgiveness...

Day 130: The wicked will fall...

Psalms 50, 53, 60, 75

What will it take for the wicked to understand that YHWH is the Creator therefore the Almighty El who is able to do all things & needs nothing from man other than their obedience & worship? For all the evidence of His awesome wonders, His amazing deeds that never cease, all His promises & blessings yet the wicked still continue in their ways that can only lead to their eternal destruction... Man's ego is certainly his downfall... Satan uses this to deceive them... Once they have a desire or envy then the enemy increases it till it becomes compulsive... They continue to feed the flesh with their worldly desires & because the spirit is starved with lack of Scriptural food, prayer, fasting & fellowship then it withers within them offering no chance of wisdom that leads to redemption & salvation... that which comes from the Holy Spirit... why? Because the Holy Spirit can only reside in the body of those who desire & walk towards righteousness... The Holy Spirit alone gives full wisdom, love, understanding & peace from YHWH but needs a clean heart to reside permanently within us... It is impossible for It to live in darkness because darkness literally and inextricably repels It...

Day 131: David's kindness misconstrued for wickedness...

2 Samuel 10; 1 Chronicles 19; Psalms 20

King David never failed in his love & mercy even towards those who presented themselves to him as enemies... Nahash, the King of Ammon died & David brought to memory his kindness... so he sent gifts of comfort to Hanun, Nahash's son... but here you can see how a dark heart & a lack of YHWH's wisdom & love can make a man be deceived by Satan... Hanun's men made him believe King David was tricking him because for them either kindness from who they saw as their enemy was unable to be conceived or that they were just wicked & loving nothing good... What a sadness that when peace is sought it is seen as war... King David experienced this kind of wickedness constantly... how burdensome on his soul it was... The Psalms is the evidence of his tribulations & persecutions but he endured because he knew YHWH his El... Psalms 20 :1 says..."May the name of the El of Jacob defend you"... The name of El the Creator, the El of Jacob is YHWH... YHWH means 'He causes to become'... Amen & Amen!!

Day 132: Praises 2 YHWH… forgive us…

Psalms 65, 66, 67, 69, 70

What beautiful scriptures from King David of his encouragement to the earth to continually give praise to YHWH… He speaks of the absolute depths of YHWH's power in mercy, love, forgiveness & peace that even the mountains, the sea, the flock, the flowers celebrate… YHWH continually blesses His righteous ones… those who fear & love Him… King David gives no misconceptions of a life led in YHWH… He exemplifies human fragility & how important it is to come before YHWH openly & honestly with our sins… It is impossible for us not to sin & thanks to Yahsah He experienced life in the flesh so the Father will always understand our shortcomings… We must not hide from Him as this will indubitably be our downfall… All praises to YHWH our Father… Redeemer… Counsellor… Protector… & Love…

Day 133: King David's terrible sin...

2 Samuel 11, 12; 1 Chronicles 20

King David was given it all... a crown... a kingdom... wives... wealth... children... Yet this wasn't enough it appears... King David strongly desired another man's wife & went as far as having him killed to get her... Bathesheba... Nathan the prophet shared a parable with King David... King David expressed abhorrence & severe punishment for the man spoken in the parable unaware that the man depicted was him... Nathan expressed YHWH's great displeasure so much that their 1st child died through sickness even though King David prayed & fasted... but YHWH forgave him & did not make him perish... but instead gave him Solomon whom "the FATHER loved"... He was also called Jedidiah... King David exemplified the carnal nature of man & how desire can cause one to sin... King David was indeed righteous & truly knew & loved the Father... but even he who YHWH anointed & has his name written in the Book of Life found himself blinded by his desire... He paid a price & it appears that he did not practice that sin or commit it again... YHWH is merciful & loving searching within the heart which is impossible for man to do... He knows his children & understands their weaknesses... but He never lets them go without chastisement or punishment... "Who He loves He chastises"... It is not clear the full extent of the role Bathesheba played but she had also committed adultery... She too paid a price by losing her 1st born child...

Day 134: Prayer of mercy & forgiveness...

Psalms 32, 51, 86, 122

Wow... King David was totally repentant... He hid nothing of his sin from YHWH... he presented himself totally naked & ashamed before His El... & our Father YHWH forgave him... yes he paid a price for his iniquity... if he didn't he would never learn the cost of sin... So too can we learn... no matter that King David sinned he never turned away from YHWH... Nathan the Prophet made King David aware that what he did was wrong... As soon as King David knew this he bowed before YHWH pleading for forgiveness... This is an example for us too... YHWH is truly merciful in His Truth & forgiving... Who else is almighty like YHWH? Who has the power to offer us life eternal in tranquillity & beauty away from the drudge, despair, trials, persecution, tribulations & loss of this world? Only Him...

Day 135: The sins of King David's sons...

2 Samuel 13, 14, 15

King David's tribulations continue as Satan continues to poison the minds of YHWH's children because of their desires... Amnon desired his sister Tamar... as a result his friend Jonadab (also his 2nd cousin) machinated against the House of King David & gave him ill advice... He consequently deceived his father, raped his sister then turned his shame & hatred on her... Absalom was unquietly furious & didn't act on it for 2 years... then Satan used this anger planting the seed of sin & Absolam murdered his brother avenging his sister's abuse... As if that wasn't enough... He burnt down his uncle's field like a petulant bully... forced his father King David to forgive him... then rallied a coup against him... King David at this time had suffered so much emotional pain & Absalom just added to it... King David had to flee his home to save his life from death at the hands of his own son... Absalom's behaviour was shameful, devious & outrageous... The wickedness & sin of man is a terrible thing... How can we be protected from this without YHWH & the guidance of His Holy Spirit? We can't... we totally need Him for ultimate survival...

Day 136: YHWH blesses forever… wickedness will not prevail…

Psalms 3, 4, 12, 13, 28, 55

King David said, "If it were enemies who reproached me then I could bear it & hide from them… but it was an equal, a companion, an acquaintance taking sweet counsel walking to the house of YHWH"… What a devastating fact of how life is for YHWH's children… YHWH blesses His children almightily but Satan has his mission set… to steal, kill & destroy the anointed & righteous… So he uses anyone who has even a slight semblance of darkness in them or insecurities…. envy, deceit, vanity, worldly desire, arrogance, idolatry, loneliness, cowardice… to name but a few…

Day 137: David mourns over Absalom...

2 Samuel 16, 17, 18

King David had to flee for his life... but thank YHWH he had men who were truly loyal to him & willing to put their own lives at risk for him... Hushai deceived Absolam to save his master King David... Absolam believed him when he said he was against King David & on his side... Word went to King David to flee the wilderness and cross the Jordan... Absolam and his men went out to war with King David's men as Hushai advised... but Absolam was caught by a tree & Joab with ten other men killed him and buried him under a pile of stones in the forest... King David mourned bitterly for his son despite his son's abhorrent disloyalty towards him... He was so pained he expressed his life to be taken instead of his son... but I don't believe he meant physically or literally... I believe he knew Absalom's soul wasn't saved and knowing this in his grief he was bargaining with his own life in order to save his son's soul... I believe this because of my own experience... not after a death but knowing that a particular person may not be saved I have offered my life to YHWH in order that their soul be saved... The prospect of everlasting damnation for someone you love is soul shuddering & devastating... It's only natural that King David as a parent would never wish it for an enemy let alone his own child...

Day 138: Merciful YHWH...

Psalms 26, 40, 58, 61, 62, 64

How merciful & great our Father YHWH is... There are so many living their lives as if YHWH does not exist in their disillusioned existence without a clue of the blessed life in YHWH... Then there are those who believe in a creator but still have no idea who He is because they follow traditions & doctrines of man or 'the church' without a clue that they are operators of iniquity & darkness... The Truth of YHWH is in Scriptures... pure & simple... His Spirit will lead you through His Word... for there you will find true salvation...

Day 139: **David reigns as king of Israel again…**

2 Samuel **19, 20, 21**

Joab gave King David an ultimatum… that he must not mourn for the enemy as if he would prefer Absolam lived & all Israel died… So King David was returned to Jerusalem by Judah & reigned… however Israel were angered & disheartened that they were not involved even though Judah is King David's family… Israel decided not to show loyalty to King David as a result…

Day 140: Hope in YHWH...

Psalms 5, 38, 41, 42

King David expressed the hardship of living a righteous life... He loved YHWH & was devoted to worshipping him... because of this the enemy was constantly persecuting him & used all areas of his life to do so... Wicked spirits know YHWH's children from birth... all the sins we have committed have been because the wicked spirits have guided us to do so but without our knowledge... So in the days of persecution those same sins that we have consequently become ashamed of is what our enemy will use to try to condemn us, criticise us then finally attempt to kill us... only the love & wisdom of YHWH can save us... because only knowing Him can we truly know ourselves... We will know we are His special peculiar people... His royal priesthood... not perfect but a precious pleasure in YHWH's sight... & when we truly know this the wicked spirits have no power over our lives... They will continue to attempt to lead us to sin but this time we are fully aware of their machinations & will rely on the love, wisdom, knowledge & forgiveness of YHWH through His Holy Spirit & the Word to avoid heeding to their iniquity & doing wrong...

Day 141: King David's legacy...

2 Samuel 22, 23; Psalms 57

What a blessing & relief YHWH was for King David... He would never have survived his persecutions & torments had it not been for YHWH... but it was his absolute unfailing faith that made it possible... He truly knew YHWH & depended on Him for EVERYTHING... every imaginable thing leaving absolutely nothing out... I am so glad I have reached that stage... Thank You YHWH for being the best Father anyone could have... 2nd to none...

Day 142: **Worship YHWH your El...**

Psalms **95, 97, 98, 99**

Psalms is King David's life experience as YHWH's anointed... It is evident that even though King David suffered persecutions & tribulations he also experienced great joy & blessings in YHWH... So much that he would sing, dance & play heartfelt melodies to our Father... This is his encouragement to us even today through the Holy Spirit of YHWH...

Day 143: Satan tempts King David to sin...

2 Samuel 24; 1 Chronicles 21, 22; Psalms 30

The fear of YHWH is understanding… King David in his flesh was tempted to sin by displaying arrogance & prideful possession… As a result a plague destroyed thousands of Israelites by the hand of YHWH's Angel… but King David pleaded his life for theirs & YHWH retracted through King David's sacrificial offer & worship… It is easy for us to be tempted by the wicked one because he infiltrates our mind subtlety making us believe the thoughts we have are generated by us… As we develop our relationship with our Father He enhances our wisdom which allows us to discern the machinations of the wicked against the pure & righteous thoughts of YHWH…

Day 144: The enemy & the Redeemer...

Psalms 108, 109, 110

I have only realised that Psalms 109 & 110 are the juxtaposed portrayal of Satan & Messiah Yahsah... Satan is truly a tormentor of the mind & his end is already a definite and determined destruction... Yahsah our Messiah is truly peace & comfort to the mind & He has no end for He is eternal... Amen!

Day 145: Solomon is King… Levites continue ministering 2 YHWH…

1 Chronicles 23, 24, 25

King David passed on his reign to his son Solomon & then divided the duties of the Levites to continue ministering to YHWH… 38,000 in all… of these 4,000 were gatekeepers & 4,000 chosen to be musicians giving sweet praises to YHWH… King David himself made the instruments… Imagine YHWH had blessed him with the gift of playing & making musical instruments amongst a host of other things… Nothing is impossible with YHWH…

Day 146: YHWH & His Holy name to be blessed forever…

Psalms 131, 138, 139, 143, 144, 145

"My mouth shall speak the praise of YHWH & all flesh shall bless His Holy name" PSALMS 145:21… YHWH Almighty never ceases to amaze me… I am almost half way through a yearly reading plan & have been in a constant, dogged battle with a man who is determined in his belief of the transliteration of the Father & the Son's names… I did not approach him but in his observance of my constant reference to Their True names he has been on a 'war path' to discredit me & my use of their names… But I have been in prayer & everyday YHWH has given me scriptures to uphold the Truth of Him & His Son… I love You Father… Thank You that You had a Son who was perfect in love, mercy, faith & obedience… May we walk on a path dedicated to You following in the steps of Yahsah our Messiah… Amen!

Day 147: Solomon reigns & builds YHWH's House...

1 Chronicles 26, 27, 28, 29; Psalms 127

King Solomon received the rights to build YHWH's House... & no other king before or after him was bestowed with such royal majesty... he was exalted exceedingly in the sight of all Israel... An abundance of gold, silver, bronze, iron, wood & silk were used for the House of YHWH... all willing donations from King David & the leaders of Israel... great banqueting & rejoicing took place as they manifested they great love for YHWH their El...

Day 148: YHWH's mercies endure forever...

Psalms 111, 112, 113, 114, 115, 116, 117, 118

Holy & precious is our Father YHWH Almighty... He is our Tower, Refuge, Comfort & Strength... There is no other like Him... He protects all His righteous who all know Him by His name... The Spirit of YHWH is the Truth & all His children know it because they know & listen to His Voice... The Father is not merely words printed on a page but the Living El residing in our heart & soul though His Holy Spirit...

Day 149: Our Rock of refuge...

1 Kings 1, 2; Psalms 37, 71, 94

Psalms 37 has wondrous, protective, reassuring words that I will share with a very special person in my life who is being afflicted by the wicked one... I know my Father YHWH will deliver her... Every day I read scriptures my faith is constantly reinforced & I am continually reassured of His love, mercy, forgiveness & the promise of an eternal existence with Him & my saviour Yahsah the Messiah... Amen!

Day 150: Blessed are those who keep YHWH's Laws...

Psalms 119

Those who with their whole heart seek YHWH will by no means be disappointed because they meditate on YHWH's commandments, statutes, precepts & words day & night... they do not wander from them & have them hidden in their hearts so they may rejoice with delight and not practice sin... Do not forget the Law of YHWH... Walk according to His Way & your salvation is secured for eternity...

Day 151: Solomon's blessing of wisdom...

1 Kings 3, 4

Oh that we should all be like Solomon... YHWH visited him in a dream & asked what He could do for him... Solomon could have asked for absolutely anything... the most money, the longest life, the prettiest woman, the biggest house... but his heart was with YHWH & to do His will... He had a pure & just heart wanting only to be a righteous & just leader... so he simply asked for WISDOM... Through his humility he was favoured in the Eyes of YHWH... So much so that YHWH gave him everything he needed & wanted in abundance & more... Solomon didn't ask for more nor did he expect it... He was respected & sought by all men from all classes & hierarchy... He set such a beautiful example as a leader & just simply as a man of YHWH Almighty... How wonderful... May I be an example of Solomon my Father that I may lead all those who I have the privilege of sharing Your Righteousness & Love with... Amen!

Day 152: Solomon blessed above all kings…

2 Chronicles 1; Psalms 72

Solomon's first desire for wisdom found absolute favour in YHWH's Eyes that YHWH blessed him more than any king before or after him… what an honour… Solomon wanted for nothing as long as he remained faithful, merciful & obedient to the Father… That is our only requirement which is all encompassed in Love…

Day 153: The Shulamite...

Song of Solomon 1, 2, 3, 4, 5, 6, 7, 8

Who is the Shulamite? The beloved's chosen... She is distinct from the Daughters of Jerusalem... She belongs to the beloved & the beloved belongs to her... She gives such a description of him & a description is given of her... She loses him & searches the city for him... She finds him & exalts him... All the while the garden & the vineyards need tending to... Her beloved dwells in the garden... "Love is as strong as death" he says... cryptic & poetic... Who can truly understand the Songs of Solomon...

Day 154: Precious Wisdom...

Proverbs 1, 2, 3

I love the Proverbs & Chapter 3 is one of my favourite... "The fear of YHWH is understanding.... When wisdom enters your heart & knowledge is pleasant to your soul then discretion & understanding will preserve & keep you"... To truly know the meaning of this is to fully understand it... Only YHWH can teach this through His Holy Spirit... It is not possible for man to... All man can do is give Words from YHWH & their own personal testimonies... Man acquires the wisdom & puts it to use for the Glory of YHWH but the True understanding of Wisdom comes directly from Him... Amen!

Day 155: Wisdom is life...

Proverbs 4, 5, 6

YHWH granted Solomon an abundance of wisdom more than any who lived before or after him... His wise sayings were known all over the globe & many travelled from far off places to hear them... These are the wise Words YHWH instilled in him that today are the Words for us also... They light the paths of YHWH's children like the sun shining bright onto a perfect day... How beautiful to know as His children we have absolutely nothing to worry about but doing right in YHWH's Eyes... Love, mercy & obedience... with YHWH always leading the way we will never be lost...

Day 156: Fear of YHWH is the beginning of Wisdom…

Proverbs 7, 8, 9

How great to be of a mind that understands how priceless the Wisdom of YHWH is… to not be driven by the things of the flesh but only by the things of the Spirit… This is no easy thing but it is simple… have the desire of your whole heart to please YHWH & He will lead you… "Trust in YHWH with your whole heart leaning not on your own understanding… but in ALL your ways acknowledge Him & He will direct your path"… This is a living fact… If you believe we have a living El then you should believe that nothing is impossible for Him to do… & the thing He most wants to do is give us ETERNAL LIFE… So let Him do it…

Day 157: The righteous vs the wicked…

Proverbs 10, 11, 12

It is quite simple… righteousness leads to everlasting life… wickedness leads to death… Wisdom gives understanding & knowledge to the righteous that brings about peace & joy… because the wicked are devoid of this wisdom their hearts are perverse… They pursue evil things… hatred, deceit, envy, greed, laziness… The wicked die through lack of wisdom… Wisdom is Yahsah the Messiah…

Day 158: Wise words...

Proverbs 13, 14, 15

Solomon was gifted with words of wisdom... so what better scriptures to read in order to gain understanding of relating to others than Proverbs... It has deep understanding of the mind, how to become a good support to others & be healthy within yourself... We are chemical beings that operate inextricably through spiritual, psychological & physiological interactions... Each has its function integral to life & deficit in any of them creates maladaptation & malfunction... The wisdom of YHWH however counsels us & brings us into healing in a way no man ever can...

Day 159: Thank You Father...

Proverbs 16, 17, 18

This is the day that You have made Father... let us all rejoice & be glad in it... How beautiful You are... The Father I never had that is with me, caring for me, leading me, exalting me, protecting me, teaching me, providing for me always & forever... How could I ever be without You? I would never want to...

Day 160: Only YHWH...

Proverbs 19, 20, 21

Solomon knew that only in our righteous walk with YHWH that we acquire His wisdom... No wickedness can befall those who walk in YHWH's Ways... When we do what is right in YHWH's Eyes He literally, practically & spiritually takes care of every one of our needs... He leaves nothing to us apart from our faith...

Day 161: **YHWH's Wisdom must be shared...**

Proverbs **22, 23, 24**

What a sad thing it is to hear a man say, "I will no longer rely on YHWH... I will go it alone"... It is a foolish man who believes that he is alone in anything he does...YHWH sees all & permits all... A man who envies the riches of the world lives only for this temporary existence & throws away the gift of eternity living as a king... It is the ego that makes a man desire the vanity of this world so others can look on him & say... "Wow... look at him... he is really doing well... isn't he great"... Yet this is temporary & amounts to nothing in the end but just an inflated ego... The One we need acknowledgement from is He that is the Master of All... Who can make or break us... Who is the giver of life & all the unimaginable riches... We just need to put Him first & wait with a glad heart...

Day 162: Solomon build's YHWH's House...

1 Kings 5, 6; 2 Chronicles 2, 3

Goodness... you can imagine how glorious, opulent, spectacular & beautiful the House of YHWH was that Solomon built in all its intricate & skilled workmanship made of the finest materials in the world... cedar wood, gold, linen, silk, precious stones... my oh my... This is what YHWH has planned for the City of Zion in the eternal life to come... these things are nothing for YHWH because He created it all... but look at the value man puts on these things making it worth more than people's lives... Man without YHWH only has concept of monetary value making it the measure of their worth... but YHWH is Spiritual & the contents of the heart is His measure of worth... All these jewels & precious materials are free as gifts from Him but not for the use of power & control... I'll wait upon Him for That Day of Tranquillity, Love & Beauty...

Day 163: Talented gifts from YHWH...

1 Kings; 2 Chronicles 4

As humans we take many things for granted... but imagine that anything we are truly good at is a gift from YHWH... Hiram, Solomon's master craftsman had a gift of working with bronze... Solomon used him to build outstanding works of art for the Temple of YHWH... When we walk according to YHWH's Ways He excels our thoughts & reveals our gifts to us... but these are to be used to enhance His Kingdom... to help bring back His people... Yes we will receive monetary gains so we are self-sufficient but this is always secondary to doing the Will of YHWH... Remember He has promised to feed, clothe & house us so this is already a given... What we need to concentrate on is following in the path of The Messiah... setting this as an example & sharing the Good news of the Gospel...

Day 164: The Ark of YHWH...

1 Kings 8; 2 Chronicles 5

The Ark of YHWH was brought home from the City of David & great rejoicing took place for 14 days... Solomon gave prayer on behalf of the whole of Israel, YHWH's children... Solomon too was aware that everyone sins & so in prayer he made request that whenever the people turned away from their sin that YHWH would give them forgiveness & peace from their trials, tribulations, pestilences, diseases, famine etc... He was a true king who cared & looked out for the people YHWH gave him to rule over...

Day 165: Give thanks to YHWH...

2 Chronicles 6, 7; Psalms 136

My YHWH He is good... & His mercies endure forever... We live in a world where people will curse The Creator for the evils, disasters & tribulations they experience or hear about... but they do not realise it is because they have turned away from Him to serve other gods (or are disobedient)... They are not acknowledging Him in their life & so He is far away from them... They do not have His blessings because by default they have refused it... "But YHWH gives food to all flesh" (PSALMS 136:25)... How great is that... yet the people who have not accepted Him have also not accepted this fact... When things are good do they say... "Let's give thanks to YHWH?" No... but when trouble is amongst them they do not hesitate in attributing it to Him... I say... "Let everything that breathes praise YHWH" — PSALMS 150:6

Day 166: Praise YHWH…

Psalms 134, 146, 147, 148, 149, 150

The Father has made an everlasting promise to all those who fear Him… He will raise up His people & humiliate the wicked those who do not accept Him as their El… Our Father YHWH is the Creator of all things… in the heaven… on the earth… in the seas… EVERYTHING GOOD… so who is man to contend with the Most High? It's ludicrous… Let everything that breathes praise YHWH…

Day 167: YHWH reminds Solomon of obedience...

1 Kings 9; 2 Chronicles 8

YHWH appears to Solomon in another dream... He confirms His promise to Solomon that He gave to his father King David but reminds him that this promise stands only if he & Israel obey His Words & do not follow other gods... Solomon was truly blessed for his faith, obedience & love towards YHWH His El...

Day 168: Be wise...

Proverbs 25, 26

Wisdom is a beautiful gift from YHWH... it is through the transforming of the mind & not being conformed to the world that sets YHWH's children apart... When we put YHWH & His Son first we are elevated in return... Our lives become richer than any precious stone can compare... Our minds can see so clearly the Works of the Holy Spirit as well as the machinations of the wicked... This surrender is necessary for unconditional faith & exclusive devotion to YHWH... People grumble... "Why should I have to give this up?... or why do I have to be controlled by a 'religion' or god?" But look at our lives... we all submit to the government... to our employers... to the law of the land... Why not to the Creator of it all who gives us the best in abundance full of true mercy, unfailing love & profound peace like none we could ever experience in this carnal world?

Day 169: True Faith brings wisdom…

Proverbs 27, 28, 29

True faith is finally knowing & not just hoping that the Creator actually exists then living your life just to please Him… You then become cleansed & healed by His Word which leads you into all wisdom… This provides your life with everything you need to live in the love, joy & peace YHWH promises… it is truly wonderful… HALLELUYAH!!!!

Day 170: Labouring for this life is vanity...

Ecclesiastes 1, 2, 3, 4, 5, 6

It is a gift when YHWH bestows riches upon His children as a reward for their labour... but that labour is doing the will of YHWH... everything else is in vain... The flesh dies, goes into the ground & rots... & all the vanity of this world is left behind for someone else... but the Spirit that is fed through the implanting of the Word & doing the will of YHWH remains forever in paradise with our Father the Most High...

Day 171: Man's all...

Ecclesiastes 7, 8, 9, 10, 11, 12

It is very very simple... "Fear YHWH & keep His commandments"... There is a great thing that man can do in his walk with YHWH... & that is reading the Scriptures... How else will we know what we need to do, how to do it & what direction we need to go in... To know YHWH is to truly fear Him... not from anxiety or terror but from awe of His omnipotence in all things wise & wonderful...

Day 172: **Solomon loses faith...**

1 Kings **10, 11;** 2 Chronicles **9**

My El... Solomon was given more wisdom & wealth than any other king that lived on earth... but he had a terrible weakness... women... & plenty of them... over a thousand... 700 wives... 300 concubines... & others in between... The desire for women was his greatest downfall & curse upon is progeny... He turned to serve the false gods of his wives & became an abomination in the Eyes of YHWH... How painful this must have been to the Father... YHWH preserved Solomon's life but his sins fell upon his children instead... YHWH had given him this warning but he chose to follow his ego & his desire... man is weak & Solomon exemplifies this... however it is not impossible to remain faithful as many others in Scriptures have proven... I know where I will stand by the grace, strength & mercy of my Father YHWH El Almighty...

Day 173: Wisdom of Proverbs...

Proverbs 30, 31

Wonderfully wise words of Proverbs... it speaks out to all situations in our lives & gives life & peace to those who take heed... I have loved reading about Solomon & the words YHWH inspired him to speak... He did fall terribly & as a result brought tribulation on his progeny... but thankfully YHWH is merciful & full of loving kindness... He forgives all those seeking it & refreshes their blessings...

Day 174: Sins of kings...

1 Kings 12, 13, 14

Why was it not enough for the kings that YHWH put in place to continue worshipping & obeying Him? How does man allow his own ego to be so compulsive & controlling that they would sin against the very Being that gives them life, favour, leadership & blessings? Man is surely foolish & stupid... greedy, hopeless & faithless... weak & selfish... so wearisome...

Day 175: YHWH forgives but chastises...

2 Chronicles 10, 11, 12

Again & again YHWH's children disobey Him... but He is so merciful that He forgives in an instance... however there is a price to pay... YHWH delivers His children but they no longer have the privilege of power to rule... they have become servants to men... they forsook the Father therefore they forsook their blessings...

Day 176: YHWH protects His Loyal Ones...

1 Kings 15; 2 Chronicles 13, 14, 15, 16

That is the long & the short of it... how faithful YHWH is... He makes a promise & He keeps it... that is much more than can be said for man... The beautiful thing is that YHWH knows we are weak... He will not keep us in tribulations as long as we confess our sins & humbly come before Him... He is so merciful & great... There is nothing impossible for Him... Imagine a million enemies came up against Asa the King of Judah & his 300,000 men... yet because of his loyalty to YHWH he was delivered from the potential slaughter... in his faith he cried out & YHWH heard him... how amazing...

Day 177: YHWH's Royal servants...

1 Kings 16; 2 Chronicles 17

How amazing the blessings of YHWH are… you would never imagine how they will come but when they do you know for sure He has given them… Judah became YHWH's chosen tribe purely because of King David's loyalty and faith… Israel were called but they desired the things of the flesh more than that of the Spirit of YHWH… They sought the false gods & were highly idolatrous… They became an abomination & a huge disappointment to YHWH… As a result they lost YHWH's protection & security leaving them open to the tribulations & devastation of the enemy… They were blinded by their own egos, their desires, their greed, their envy & their self-obsessions that they forsook their salvation & promise of eternal paradise with the Almighty & His Son… They also forsook true peace & joy in this world…

Day 178: Eliyah vs Jezebel...

1 Kings 17, 18, 19

Jezebel was the daughter of a Sidonian king who married Omri King of Israel... He turned his back on YHWH & served the Baals influenced by Jezebel... YHWH raised Eliyah the prophet who came to Ahab prophesying drought & famine... As a result YHWH instructed Eliyah to remain at the brook by The Jordan to preserve his life from the hands of King Ahab & Jezebel... YHWH took care of all his needs... He touched the hearts of those who feared Him so Eliyah never starved... even birds & angels came to feed him... Eliyah feared for his life & spent 40 days fasting in the wilderness... Over 400 prophets were slain at the hands of Jezebel that only Eliyah one remained... YHWH anointed Elisha to serve after Eliyah but he became his servant first... The prophets' duty was heavy for Eliyah to carry but YHWH did not forsake him... Eliyah learned to be alone with The Father... he was homeless, hungry, lonely & fearful through various moments in his life serving YHWH but he never lost his faith... even through the drought & famine He trusted in YHWH & believed every Word of our Father... YHWH promised to take care of him & Eliyah stood firm in His Words... He proved to be a loyal & worthy servant of YHWH...

Day 179: Sins of the fathers fall on the sons...

1 Kings 20, 21

Ahab was granted mercy by YHWH and won two wars against King Ben-Hadad of Syria in an almighty & miraculous way... But Ahab's intimacy with Jezebel caused him to sin greatly... Jezebel had Naboth a man of YHWH killed because Ahab wanted his vineyard to make a garden... he couldn't even eat because Naboth refused to hand it over... For this evil deed YHWH sent Eliyah with a prophesy that both Ahab & Jezebel will be eaten by dogs & Ahab's posterity will be cut off... Ahab repented mightily & YHWH showed him mercy... however YHWH swore that his sons would bear the curse therefore carrying the sins of their father... I would believe they would not be doing good themselves and following in the continual sinful ways of their forefathers... YHWH would not condemn His Children who are doing good... look how He showed mercy to King Ahab much less...

Day 180: Foolishness of kings...

1 Kings 22; 2 Chronicles 18

King Ahab was given an ultimate position of power on earth by YHWH's Hands... but like the kings before & many of the Israelites he sinned against YHWH & chose to serve other gods... His ego blinded him, deafened him & fooled him so he could not hear & accept the truth of his fate when spoken through Micaiah the Prophet... Imagine YHWH's angelic spirits persuaded the 400 prophets to lie to King Ahab & because his heart was darkened & unable to discern the things of the Holy Spirit he condemned Micaiah instead, went out to war & died... He even attempted to prevent his predicted demise by disguising himself... he attempted to make himself more powerful than the Father... What a fool he was... All the blessings YHWH promised him yet it was not enough... He allowed Satan instead to deceive him and fool his mind...

Day 181: Sins of kings continue...

2 Chronicles 19, 20, 21, 22, 23

Kings... nobles... men... all weak & egotistical... They experience the Power of YHWH's glory & blessings yet to satisfy their own desires they quite easily turn their backs on the Father & so ultimately condemn their selves... It is ludicrous & they don't seem to learn from what has taken place before them... It is so important to keep a check of our thoughts & feelings... are they in line with YHWH's ways? Is what we think & feel pleasing to YHWH? Then we need to pray to Him to help us to think, feel & do what is right in His Eyes because we do not have the power to do it without Him... no one has... & that is the mistake of man... believing they can manage their own lives... But YHWH is the Creator of all... He gives life & He takes it away... Ultimately our destiny is with Him & if we choose to serve ourselves as serving other gods then He forsakes us so we are left at the mercy of the enemy who will eventually kill, steal & destroy us in any heinous way possible...

Day 182: Downfall of Jacob's twin Esau...

Obadiah 1

Imagine Jacob & Esau came from the same seed yet only Jacob received YHWH's blessing whilst Esau was hated... It doesn't seem feasible but yet this is the way it still is today... division in the family... those who stand firm in the faith of YHWH living according to His Ways & those who are deceived by the desires of their own heart following their futile power mocking the ones who humble themselves to YHWH... Theirs is a bitter end & all the glory goes to YHWH's children... those who have Him as their True El...

Day 183: Eliyah rises in glory...

2 Kings 1, 2, 3, 4

Eliyah was a loyal servant of YHWH... so much so YHWH sent a chariot of fire to collect him when his time on earth was over... He did not experience death as all other men have... his was a majestic & glorious exit from this world... He was indeed truly special in the Eyes of YHWH... doing great works regardless of the risks & threats... Elisha was given the mantle of Eliyah & continued with twice the power of the Spirit as he had earnestly requested... He went on to perform great miracles & spoke great prophecies... YHWH touched the heart of His people so Elisha was looked after in his ministry...

Day 184: Elisha... another great prophet...

2 Kings 5, 6, 7, 8

When Eliyah had spoken to Elisha telling him he was leaving to go to His Maker he said that if he saw him go up in a chariot of fire his request of a double portion of his spirit would be given... & so said so done... Elisha witnessed Eliyah departing & therefore performed amazingly great works for YHWH... He prophesied many calamities against nations... against kings... He forewarned & aided YHWH's children & remained faithful...

Day 185: **Prophets appear insane...**

2 Kings **9, 10, 11**

It is not the first time in Scriptures where prophets in their ministry of prophesy are perceived as crazy... this is no different today with YHWH's children... YHWH has given us a message for the whole nation... He is real & salvation belongs to Him... But when we give this message to those who do not have the spirit of YHWH they mock, scoff & proclaim us as not having sound minds... oh the irony...

Day 186: The Temple rebuilt...

2 Kings 12, 13; 2 Chronicles 24

Israel did not stop in its sinful ways... Judah still remained favourable in YHWH's Eyes due to His covenant with David... Some of the Kings of Judah were still sinning but Joash who was only 7 years old when he started his reign did right in YHWH's Eyes... He restored the Temple of YHWH & the hearts of His People... It was a constant battle to keep the worshipping of false gods away from their presence and continue to admonish the people to follow the commands of YHWH... They paid a price for forsaking The Father... He forsook them so they were left open to the attack of their enemies... It is the same today... people complaining about the disasters & affliction & blaming YHWH... but do they even accept Him as their Father & Master putting Him first? Are they allowing Him to rebuild the temple within & therefore receive the protection that is promised?

Day 187: Stiff-necked kings...

2 Kings 14; 2 Chronicles 25

Still they didn't learn from their fathers before them... Satan is so great at articulation, cunning & deception that great kings who have reaped the numerous blessings of YHWH turn away from Him & start to serve the false gods... It never ceases to astonish me but it is evident that our only protection from Satan is the Word of YHWH to cleanse us... Our true dedication & loyalty must be to living a life pleasing to YHWH in order to receive His Holy Spirit of Truth... It is this Truth & our desire to remain in YHWH's favour that will save us from the snares of Satan... It is the purity of our hearts that will keep us in line with His Spirit remembering that chasing after the things of this world is vanity because it is ephemeral... temporary... but longing for the things of YHWH is perpetual leading to an eternal life in paradise with our loving Creator & His Son Yahsah the Messiah... That is my true desire more than anything else... what is yours?

Day 188: Jonah's mission...

Jonah 1, 2, 3, 4

A great account of a man of YHWH given a message but too afraid or intolerant to pass it on... He runs away to sea but the Power of YHWH follows him... He cannot escape that which YHWH has purposed... so much so YHWH excels the minds of the men on board the ship so they realise why they are facing shipwreck... They too are faced with their own plight & acknowledge YHWH as the Almighty making or renewing vows & giving sacrifices... When YHWH has a purpose for our lives we can run but He will bring us back full circle so we realise our purpose otherwise we will perish... just like Jonah would have if he didn't make prayer & make good... He will give insight to others to ensure that what He purposes will be done... The sailors witnessed the Almighty Power & Mercy of YHWH & Jonah accepted his fate... He too experienced the Mercy of YHWH & so carried out the work he was initially instructed to do... However again the mercilessness of the flesh consumed him & YHWH in His loving kindness & His mercy demonstrated why He did not destroy Nineveh using an analogy... YHWH truly demonstrates patience & understands that in our flesh we cannot always understand the things of the Spirit... That's why YHWH is constantly willing to teach us so we too can shine a light like Him to those we encounter...

Day 189: Pride kills the spirit…

2 Kings 15; 2 Chronicles 26

As a humans we are susceptible to arrogance and pride when we have achieved great things… but these achievements are by YHWH's grace… Being mindful is the key to keeping our humility in place remembering we are nothing without YHWH and that He causes all things to become… Pride always comes before a fall…

Day 190: Isaiah prophesies YHWH's vengeance...

Isaiah 1, 2, 3, 4

Oh how YHWH is so disappointed & angry with the continual sinning of Israel that He has pronounced their fate through Isaiah... unless they turn away from the worship of idols & their evil doings He will destroy them through the Spirit of Judgement & the Spirit of Burning... He will purge the filth from amongst His People & those remaining shall dwell in holiness...

Day 191: Israel in trouble...

Isaiah 5, 6, 7, 8

Isaiah was chosen as a prophet even though he felt he was unclean & unworthy... He was made clean via an angel & he courageously accepted his ministry... The message he brought to the Israelites was severe... It was the most pertinent & prolific of all the messages given by the Holy Prophets... He proclaimed the Coming of Yahsah The Messiah as well as the doom & destruction that was to come before this advent... Israel had really become filthy & a cleaning up process was in order... The only thing to save them was to return to YHWH with humility & forgiveness...

Day 192: Punishment on Israel & Judah...

Amos 1, 2, 3, 4, 5

What a clear message Amos had for YHWH's People in regards to their transgression and the imminent downfall should they not heed... Disaster was also prophesied to those nations who abused YHWH's People... YHWH says not a matter will take place unless He has revealed it to His chosen & He needs prophets to prophesy these matters...

Day 193: **Israel's doom...**

Amos **6, 7, 8, 9**

Israel surely has made The Father unhappy... Imagine everything that you have has been given by our Father... then you turn round & rebuke Him... ignore Him & disrespect Him... going off to give glory to some other king whose power is no way near as great as The Father... You continue to conduct yourself in nasty, sinful ways... It is no wonder the Creator is unhappy & angry... This was not His intention for His People... He knows only beauty & knows man is his own downfall by allowing himself to be led astray by the wicked one... YHWH says He will cause a famine... not of the physical food but the spiritual word... Now is the time to be in Scriptures because when that famine comes & we have not been in The Word then the wicked will deceive from left, right & centre using crafty words & we will not be able to discern the Truth from the deception because 1. we will not have The Word in us & 2. the Word will be nowhere to be found... Be in the Word now so when the day comes It can be retrieved from within your heart, mind & soul...

Day 194: The Messiah's Coming proclaimed...

2 Chronicles 27; Isaiah 9, 10, 11, 12

Isaiah was given the prophecy of The Messiah's birth & His Salvation for all men... Though YHWH is angry He still has His arm outstretched to receive anyone who asks for forgiveness & repents... Everything happening in those times of Isaiah is happening now... These are not just stories... these are actual events mirroring those of today... If we are not found with the Light then we are still in darkness & our end will be destruction... Walk in the Light and with the Light while it can be found so we can remain in the Light for eternity...

Day 195: YHWH delights in mercy...

Micah 1, 2, 3, 4, 5, 6, 7

What an almighty El we serve in YHWH... Despite all our transgressions because His delight is in mercy He will always have compassion for us... What a wonderful promise & assurance... He knows how difficult life is for those who are truly loyal to Him... but for those who delight in evil He has sent His prophets to prophesy their end... even those amongst His People He has given an ultimatum... YHWH loves us otherwise why would He have made us & given us a beautiful planet to live on & beautiful people to share it with... All the beauty & love we have within comes from Him & that's why we all need to acknowledge Him to gain salvation & eternal residence in Paradise... There is no compromise... It's Him or nothing... because without Him the susceptibility to evil is prevalent & more inclined to be activated... With Him He has fought & won the war against evil... therefore our belief & exercising of faith in Him is what protects us...

Day 196: Today's false religions...

2 Kings 16, 17; 2 Chronicles 28

This is an elucidating chapter... It chronicles Israel's split from serving the True Hebrew El YHWH to the beginning of serving the false gods that are still present today... There are many religions prevalent that do not accept the One True El but follow images of false gods & polytheism... The heart of man can be so arrogant & foolish... but it is purely to do with their desire... If we have a desire to serve YHWH first & foremost then it is through this desire that YHWH will guide & lead us because it is most important to us... But if our desire is of the fleshly things then it is through this that we will be lead & we all know the things of the flesh belong to Satan... the things of the flesh enhances the ego & all the ego is interested in is making itself feel more important above others... even above YHWH...

Day 197: Destruction of Satan...

Isaiah 13, 14, 15, 16, 17

Here lies the destruction of Satan & all who follow Him... that includes even those who may not have willingly accepted Satan but have openly refuted YHWH & The Messiah... These include Babylon, Assyria, Moab & those without the Spirit of YHWH... Theirs is total destruction & mercy is given only to YHWH's Children... Hell will be waiting to receive them... woe if you are one of them... The beauty is YHWH is giving every opportunity to everyone to accept salvation while He can be found so that no one can say He is not merciful, righteous & full of loving kindness when that time comes...

Day 198: Isaiah's revelation...

Isaiah 18, 19, 20, 21, 22

Isaiah walked naked amongst the nation for 3 years as a sign of what was to come to those sinning against YHWH... Egypt, Ethiopia, Assyria, Jerusalem... They all sinned... they all fell... but YHWH cleansed & gave them back the blessing... only after the rot was taken out so the beauty remained... What a difficult, tremendous & disturbing time it must have been for Isaiah... He remained faithful to carry the Prophecies of YHWH... You can imagine how he was received by the nation... He would have been taunted, ridiculed, scoffed at, derided & mocked... But he stood firm... Absolutely amazing... such fortitude...YHWH knows that whoever He chooses to do His work they will deliver...

Day 199: Take heed & prosper…

Isaiah 23, 24, 25, 26, 27

My goodness… Isaiah had a message for YHWH's children & the nation… but that message still stands today… Those in the Spirit will see the goodness, glory & great salvation of YHWH our Father who never fails in His Promise to those who walk according to His Ways… But for those NOT in the Spirit they will interpret this message as merciless & controlling with their minds full of lofty thoughts & pride… It is not YHWH's will that any should perish but that all should come to repentance… He is the Most Upright… He is fair & just… He is a bringer of peace… He is a comforter full of loving kindness…

Day 200: Hezekiah's devote loyalty...

2 Kings 18; 2 Chronicles 29, 30, 31; Psalms 48

Hezekiah had a wonderful heart towards YHWH... It took several generations for a King of Judah like him to reign since King David... He restored Israel & Judah therefore bringing them back into YHWH's protective custody... But not all of Israel came... only those it appears from Asher, Manasseh & Zebulon it stated...

Day 201: Israel's infidelity...

Hosea 1, 2, 3, 4, 5, 6, 7

I have really come to understand the metaphor of Israel playing the harlot & adulteress… YHWH prepared Israel as a bride for Him… However she was not contented with our Father YHWH so went to seek another… fornicated… led others astray… & became an abomination… She was unfaithful to YHWH… As a result YHWH sent the prophet Hosea to give understanding of their sins, the chastisement to come & the subsequent healing… He instructed him to take a harlot, marry her & beget children for a sign of what is to become of Jezreel… In order that YHWH's children can come back to Him once they have sinned they have to experience pain & tribulation… in that way they will have a need to call upon The Creator & only then through healing will they see the true glory of YHWH's mercy, righteousness, justice & love… If this process did not take place all would be lost forever cause it's only the true knowledge & understanding of YHWH that can save us…

Day 202: Ephraim & Israel's devastation...

Hosea 8, 9, 10, 11, 12, 13, 14

Ephraim & Israel have made a grave error... they have decided to go and worship gods who can never save them... YHWH is the Only Saviour that exist through Yahsah the Messiah... There is no other saviour besides Him... The futility of man will ultimately lead to his destruction... Anyone who believes they can lead their own life is destined to be destroyed... They may call upon YHWH but if He does not come first in your life then you may as well be serving Baal... To truly know YHWH is to worship Him in Spirit & Truth walking earnestly in His Ways with a true desire in your heart to live according to His Will...

Day 203: YHWH's anger...

Isaiah 28, 29, 30

Our Father YHWH is angry with His people... & it's not surprising... They go about on their own volition following the things of this world believing this is YHWH's intention... not understanding that our focus in life is to live according to His will... chasing primarily & with integrity the things of The Spirit & not the things of the flesh... It is being able to be content with what YHWH has purposed for us... not being anxious for anything but knowing that YHWH will always provide what we need... Many blame Satan for the things they want but don't get... If YHWH wants us to have it no one can stop us having it... Let us be content with what we have & have a desire to please YHWH first... not ourselves... When we put YHWH first... He puts us first... How can that which has been created question the Creators power & ability then make the decision to walk according to their own counsel & way? Woe to those who do...

Day 204: YHWH feels pain...

Isaiah 31, 32, 33, 34

You can really understand the pain that YHWH feels watching His creation sin... He is real & everything about us is an image of Him... So if we are emotional & psychological beings then so is He... & because He is a Spiritual Being so are we... The only difference is we are in physical form here on the earth just as YAHSAH the Messiah became when He was on earth... So just like a Father He feels the pain of His children's rejection, disobedience & foolishness...

Day 205: **The haughty shall fall...**

Isaiah **35, 36**

The arrogance & haughtiness of man is his downfall... Satan deceives people through their own egos... The more a person believes he is great above most or all the more Satan will convince him that he is invincible & indispensable... Big mistake because unless you are humbling yourself to YHWH giving Him exclusive devotion then you are mere vanity, dispensable, fragile, weak, inadequate & doomed for destruction... YHWH is the True El & Creator & does not favour self-exultation... Pride is a sin & indubitably comes before a fall... Humility is a worthy trait that brings warmth, peace, love & joy to those who possess it... "YHWH resists the proud but gives grace to the humble" — JAMES 4:6

Day 206: Hezekiah's life enhanced...

Isaiah 37, 38, 39; Psalms 76

It can be said that YHWH will let His chosen know when their death is imminent... Hezekiah was stricken by a tumour that was going to take his life very soon... As he faced his mortality he cried bitterly to YHWH & YHWH heard him... Because of his faithfulness, his loyalty & his obedience YHWH healed him and enhanced his life for a further 15 years... how amazing... However Isaiah prophesied that his progeny would be captive to Babylon... Hezekiah was just thankful that for the remainder of his lifetime on earth he would experience peace...

Day 207: YHWH proclaims His Son...

Isaiah 40, 41, 42, 43

Isaiah 42 gives an indubitable reference of YHWH the Father calling upon His Son Yahsah the Messiah in preparation of sending Him as a Light to the nation... The trinity does not exist... well not in the sense the churches have tried to lead us to believe... The Messiah & The Father are separate beings & the Holy Spirit is the ultimate Power that comes from YHWH... All three work together as if one but they are not one in form... To accept that they are one is to say The Messiah has the Power of the Father & is the Almighty... & that YHWH has succumbed to the lesser power of a Son... YHWH is not an El of confusion & it's clear to see that the trinity is a confusing & erroneous concept... YHWH exacts exclusive devotion & this would be impossible if we worshipped The Messiah & Him as the same...

Day 208: No other El but YHWH…

Isaiah 44, 45, 46, 47, 48

There is only One El… YHWH the Most High… The Almighty… The Father's name YaHWaH means "He causes to become"… His Son's name Yahsah means "Yah is salvation"… To know Him is to know this… No other can save us but YHWH… The Messiah Yahsah came to show The Way… He exemplified the way in which we should walk… with obedience in mercy & love… The Messiah carried the sins of the world… He accepted the Work His Father instructed in the face of & ultimately to His death… He carried the full burden of pain, rebuke, rejection & derision all for love… all for us… I love my Father & I love my Messiah… I need to share the truth & love of YHWH with those who do not know Him fully as well as those who have chosen to worship idols & false gods…

Day 209: YHWH... our refuge & strength...

2 Kings 19; Psalms 46, 80, 135

We truly are nothing without YHWH... The nations & those not believing in Him go about their day in the own futile power believing they are in control of their lives... but they are not... If one does not accept YHWH as the True & Living El in order that He may direct their path then by default they have invited Satan to direct them instead... So whilst they believe their thoughts are their own & they are in charge of their lives it is Satan planting thoughts that in turn guides their feelings and drives their behaviour... They don't know all this because they have rejected & refuted the Living El... Therefore YHWH has caused their eyes, ears & heart to be shut so they have no sight, no hearing or any understanding of the spiritual things of YHWH... I am thankful He called me & chose me so that I may reside with my Father who is indubitably my refuge & my strength...

Day 210: The Messiah redeems on YHWH's behalf...

Isaiah 49, 50, 51, 52, 53

Isaiah speaks predominantly of the coming of Yahsah The Messiah... YHWH tells him that a Saviour will come out of Jerusalem to bring His People back... Yahsah took on all our sins... was chastised for the sake of our peace... & by His wounding we have the chance to be healed... What love the Father & the Son have for us... for the whole world... Our El is offering everything we could possibly need but the flesh of the people want the vain desires of the heart... these have no real value and will eventually disappear... Instead they refute the worthiness & riches that YHWH offers which are priceless & perpetual...

Day 211: YHWH's promises never fail...

Isaiah 54, 55, 56, 57, 58

Isaiah gives prophecy of this time... & YHWH our Father sets a list of promises to those who are loyal to Him... The time is now for every one that breathes to accept YHWH as their El & walk according to His Way...

Day 212: Zion's glory...

Isaiah 59, 60, 61, 62, 63

What a wonderful eternity with our Father & His Son we have to look forward to... When you think of the vanities of this life they are nothing compared to what YHWH our Father has in store for us... The only things worth caring about in this world are people... & helping them all to come into the salvation of YHWH... that's the most important thing as YHWH's Children that we can do for anyone... that is a true & ultimate rendition of love... Things don't matter but people do... but not for the sake of our own happiness but for the sake of His Love for us... this is a deeper & eternally sustaining love...

Day 213: People of Zion...

Isaiah 64, 65, 66

YHWH is the Potter & we are the clay... Every one of us has been made by His Hands... but He has a Chosen People... those reserved as Zion... YHWH's chosen are those who wait on Him, who rejoices in doing righteousness & who remember His Ways... He shows mercy to those who are poor & contrite in heart... Are you one of the People of Zion?

Day 214: Then & today...

2 Kings 20, 21

Israel sinned greatly against YHWH the Most High by serving & worshipping false gods... Today is no different... There are so many religions... so many denominations... Even within so-called 'Christianity' there is division, discrepancy & differences... What then separates them all? There's Anglicans, Catholics, 7th Day Adventists, Jehovah's Witnesses, Baptists, Mormons, Methodists & many more... What distinguishes these from one another? Only their man made doctrines because all fall short of the Truth... The Messiah Yahsah did not teach any of these religions or denominations... He taught the Way of YHWH His Father... & that Way is found only in Scriptures by the ultimate & True guidance of the Holy Spirit... Do not be led by the doctrines of today's churches because they are in essence no different to the worship of Baal & the false gods of Israel... Search hard, long & deep for the Truth & do not rely on the 'churches' to give it to you... Unfortunately they have their own agendas & it is not according to the Way of YHWH... they operate ultimately as a business... Whilst the churches of 'Christendom' is the starting point of everyone seeking El, including mine, do not let it be the end... The True Church is worshipping in Spirit & Truth... knowing YHWH the Only True El & His Son Yahsah The Messiah who He sent forth — JOHN 17 Remember YHWH's Children are a peculiar people, a chosen race, a royal priesthood (1 PETER 2)... We are set apart from the world & it is clear & evident to see... This challenge takes fortitude, diligence, deep desire, absolute loyalty, exclusive devotion & a true love for YHWH The Creator...

Day 215: Hezekiah's loyalty... Manasseh's humility...

2 Chronicles 32, 33

From both these Kings of Judah we can learn valuable lessons & examples of how we should be in YHWH's Eyes... Hezekiah pleased YHWH almost as much as King David... He did what was right, good & true before YHWH his El... As a result he prospered greatly... He was even given 15 more years of life on his death bed due to his dedication, devotion & loyalty to YHWH... Manasseh his son however sinned greatly against YHWH but he reigned 55 years thankfully because in that time he was taken captive by the King of Assyria... As a result he pleaded with YHWH & humbled himself fully & YHWH heard his prayers & delivered him... How utterly beautiful, merciful & loving... After all the sinning & abhorrence Manasseh had done against YHWH in one earnest plea for forgiveness YHWH forgave him... & from then to his death Manasseh turned from serving the foreign & false gods to going back to serving YHWH the rest of his days... As a Leader of YHWH's people he also ordered Israel to serve the True El...

Day 216: YHWH's anger towards wickedness...

Nahum 1, 2, 3

YHWH is so angry with the wickedness in this world not just then in Nineveh... Wickedness comes in many forms & leads to destruction... But YHWH is merciful... should the perpetrator repent of them then YHWH will forgive him & give him glory of salvation & eternal life in Paradise... Why be wicked? Because Satan has surely deceived them... Even the chosen he will attempt to deceive... He is more subtle than people can imagine... Our only defence is the Scriptures but only when read in Spirit & Truth through exclusive worship to the Only True El & with the accurate knowledge of all things given by the Holy Spirit...

Day 217: King Josiah worthy...

2 Kings 22, 23; 2 Chronicles 34, 35

King Josiah was favoured in the Eyes of YHWH... He walked all the days of his life according to the commands of The Father... He rid the country of the abominations of false idols & instructed the Israelites to give True Worship to YHWH... As a result his days on earth were in peace... He was obedient & his deeds were remarkable that no king before or after had a heart like his... His laments were etched in history to celebrate him...

Day 218: Woe to the wicked...

Zephaniah 1, 2, 3

My El... He has spoken... & woe to those who do not take heed... Our El is not asking much but justice & righteousness... However the very nature of man is flesh & sinful having a desire for the things of this world... The key & the ultimate road to salvation is practicing & striving for perfection in the things of the Spirit... these are love, joy, peace, patience, faithfulness, kindness, goodness, gentleness & self-control — GALATIANS 5... As long as we are in meditation with YHWH our Father, reading our Scriptures daily & being doers of His Word not just hearers doing all this with pure love for the Father, His Son & His creations then His Holy Spirit works in us moving & guiding us to do what is right... It starts with our thoughts of which we have the power to manage with YHWH's Wisdom found only in the Scriptures interpreted by Holy Spirit... All we need is a zeal & a desire... YHWH does the rest... Amazing...

Day 219: Jeremiah... Prophet before his birth...

Jeremiah 1, 2, 3

Jeremiah was one of the most courageous & boldest prophets that ever lived... YHWH formed & ordained him before his entrance into this world... YHWH set before him a great & fierce mission... to bring back His People from their evil ways... their backsliding and their worshipping of lifeless gods in the form of "stones & trees"... YHWH is embittered by them forsaking the fountain of living water for the cisterns they carved out that are unable to hold any water... Senseless acts has been & is still being committed by those YHWH has called... Jeremiah's words are as pertinent today as they were in the days of our ancestors... All YHWH requires is true repentance... to turn back & face Him with a contrite heart & a desire to please Him...

Day 220: Turn back Israel & Judah… it's not too late…

Jeremiah 4, 5, 6

Oh my El… destruction is at the door… & we know it's soon… all the signs are here… What can we who are loyal to YHWH do? We can exemplify His Son & show love giving glad tidings of the good news… Let the nations see in us the Love of YHWH that is His Son… loyal, obedient, humble, peaceful, full of loving-kindness… These fruits conquer the wicked & their deeds in a way that nothing else can… therefore giving great opportunity for them to repent & turn back into the arms of our gracious, righteous, merciful & loving Father…

Day 221: The House of YHWH...

Jeremiah 7, 8, 9

YHWH is the Hebrew name of the True El... the Creator of this universe... "Has this house which is called by My name become a den of thieves?" The world has defiled the Father by removing His name from Scriptures... They have instead chosen to call Him by a name that isn't His... Jehovah is a name man has given him... just like Jesus is not the true name of Messiah but Yahsah... YHWH pronounced YaHWaH means 'He causes to become' & derives from the Hebrew verb 'hawah' meaning to become... Yahsah means 'Yah is salvation'... He came to proclaim the good news of His Father... It is understandable that these are the true names as they have meanings relevant, pertinent & integral to our faith & journey with the Father & the Son... The real question is when worshipping in the name of Jehovah & Jesus who are you really worshipping... Search for wisdom & truth as if you are searching for buried treasure — PROVERBS 2:4,5... Do not just accept what you are told by the churches of this world... They have their own hidden agendas... & trust me for most it does not involve your spiritual well-being... All praises to YHWH our Father & His Son Yahsah the Messiah who He sent forth with knowledge & a promise of eternal salvation in paradise — JOHN 17:3

Day 222: Love for YHWH... my El...

Jeremiah 10, 11, 12, 13

Thank You Father... my loving & merciful El... I am nothing without You & would never ever want to be without You... There is nothing this world could offer me that would take me away from You... why? Because the material things of this world are transient giving temporary joy and false hope... It will eventually disintegrate & become nothing... But everything with You oh Creator of this universe is eternal, everlasting, magnificent, true & will never fail... You created all things why should I leave You to worship someone or something else that has no more power than me? There is no one else that has power greater than me but You & Your Son (& your ministering angels of course)... You yourself have said, "Do not be afraid of them... for they cannot do evil nor can they do any good"... Father I walk confidently & boldly in Your name... I boast & take pride in You... YHWH El Almighty The True El who created the heavens & the earth... & who ultimately sent forth His Only Son Yahsah the Messiah to give humanity one last chance of salvation before it is too late... You definitely love us just as a Father should... You are giving warnings just as a Father should... You are disciplining us just as a Father should... You are protecting us, giving us peace, bringing us into joy, uniting Your Family... just as a Father does... & getting rid of anything contaminating & toxic... just as a Father must...

Day 223: YHWH today...

Jeremiah 14, 15, 16, 17

Oh that all the people of the earth would acknowledge that there is a Creator of the world... & come to know that He is YHWH... There would be no pain or suffering... no disturbance of peace... But unfortunately most have inherited the traits of their forefathers... giving in to their flesh & the futility of it... actually believing they are their own power & their own god... Not at all aware that because they have not recognised or acknowledge the Creator that Satan is their power & their god planting their thoughts & driving their behaviours... Because they have not accepted YHWH as their El they lack the wisdom they need to discern between the thoughts that are theirs, those which are YHWH's & that which belongs to the father of deceit... What we need to do is so simple... but because the heart of the wicked & unbelieving is cold, dark, hard & closed simplicity becomes complex, complicated, confusing & contemptible... so that in the end they are cut off from the Glorious Promise of our Father YHWH & His ultimate protection...

Day 224: Jeremiah's persecution...

Jeremiah 18, 19, 20, 21, 22

Could any of us be a Jeremiah today? Indeed Jeremiah was fashioned from birth to become a great prophet on a great mission... Never-the-less his journey was thwart with derision, mockery, imprisonment & persecutions from all those around who refuted the Word of YHWH to walk according to their own fleshly ways... Jeremiah is to be admired greatly... He accepted his commission as a soldier & trusted implicitly & explicitly in the Father... It is the Kings of Judah that YHWH condemned that needed to be fearful... yet them & their subjects continued to sin & reject the Words of YHWH... So be it... They are indeed fools... & just as today many lament because of the tragedies that befall them... YHWH has said if they choose not to serve Him but go after the false gods & walk according to the desires of their heart then He shall turn His back on them & leave them in the hands of their enemies... It is their choice... Life or death...

Day 225: Doom, desolation & disaster...

Jeremiah 23, 24, 25

Jeremiah had a severely depressing mission... His task to forewarn the whole world of the impending doom, desolation & disaster that is to fall upon all those who refuse to listen to the Word of YHWH & continue in their sinful ways... Jeremiah had to take his prophesy to the shepherds also & warn them of how great their devastation will be for leading YHWH's sheep astray...

Day 226: False prophets...

Jeremiah 26, 27, 28, 29

YHWH raises prophets to deliver His Word... so when false prophets go out in His Name theirs is a devastating end... To know the truth is to know YHWH... However even the elect & the chosen can be deceived... It is therefore integral to be in Scriptures daily praying always to The Father YHWH to send His Holy Spirit to give interpretation & accurate knowledge... Do not just rely on study bibles or the mouth of others... Put all things in prayers & wait upon YHWH... The Father commands all things... even his Own Son... We are to take example of His Son's obedience... Everything we need to know is in the Scriptures... The one thing to be aware of is the names of the Father & the Son... remember they have been transliterated... Their True Hebrew names are YHWH & Yahsah... & NOT Jesus or Jehovah... False prophets have brought these names prophesying a lie... These are serious times for the Children of YHWH... there is no time for complacency... Now is the time to work out our salvation with fear & trembling...

Day 227: YHWH's Redemption...

Jeremiah 30, 31

YHWH is our El... & we are His People... He is writing a New Covenant... He will put it in our minds & write it on our hearts... & no more will we teach each other because from the least to the greatest we will all know YHWH our El... He will forgive all our sins & remember them no more... How absolutely wonderful for those who cling onto their faith in the Father & remain loyal... When YHWH promises He never fails... May You always find pleasure in Your People Oh YHWH... & may we always seek You first above all things... Continue to guide & help us to do the things that are right in Your Eyes walking always in Your Holy Spirit whilst denying the desires of the flesh... Only You can do this for us... In You I shall remain...

Day 228: Promises...

Jeremiah 32, 33, 34

It is certainly a difficult road we walk when we make a conscious & loyal decision to walk with The Messiah alongside His Father (MATTHEW 7:14)... But it is also the most joyous & peaceful because only YHWH Almighty can offer absolute solutions to our trials & give us blessings when we surmount them... We will all go through trials & tribulations but all we need to do is stand firm in our walk of faith & trust in YHWH explicitly that He will do for His People that which He promises... deliver us... However let it be without doubting (JAMES 1:2-8)...

Day 229: **Obedience & oppression...**

Jeremiah **35, 36, 37**

Obedience & oppression appear to go hand in hand when pertaining to our faith in the Father... Jeremiah, the Prophets before, the Prophets after & then our Messiah all experienced this dichotomy... They had a very difficult mission & remained obedient... The Messiah exemplified perfection through His ultimate obedience... They neither failed or faltered remaining loyal to the end... How many of us could withstand the oppression from the world because of our obedience to the Father? How far are we prepared to go or how much are we prepared to suffer to remain obedient to YHWH before we start to deny Him?

Day 230: Judah... the Remnant...

Jeremiah 38, 39, 40; Psalms 74, 79

Who is Judah? They are the chosen of YHWH because of King David's exclusive devotion to Him... He sanctified & separated them from the rest of Israel... So too the Levites... But we serve such a loving & merciful El that He also extended His salvation to the Gentiles... that is the rest of the world... So whether we are Remnants, Israelites or Gentiles we ALL have the opportunity for salvation & everlasting peace with Our Father YHWH El Almighty & His Son Yahsah the Messiah...

Day 231: Be warned... take heed...

2 Kings 24, 25; 2 Chronicles 36

What tragedy befell Jerusalem... but YHWH our El forewarned them... not once, twice or thrice but many many times... Over generations He sent out His Prophets to prophesy the destruction if they did not repent & return to Him... & still His People's necks got stiffer & their hearts harder until ultimately they paid the price... famine, slaying, captivity... young, old, women, man, children... None was spared who had gone against walking with The Father... It is no different today... YHWH has sent out the ultimate Prophet... His Son Yahsah Messiah... Those who choose to oppose Him & walk according to their own ways & the desires of their heart will indubitably experience the fate of Jerusalem... YHWH is merciful & loving... He is forewarning... Nothing evil or a heart not for Him can exist amongst His Righteousness & Holiness... It is naturally impossible hence the imbalance & imperfection we face today...

Day 232: Cry out to YHWH...

Habakkuk 1, 2, 3

Nothing is impossible for YHWH... No matter what we may be facing YHWH El Almighty hears the cries of His Loyal Ones... We can plead our case at any time... We can ask Him questions respectfully... I love my Father... He is the Omnipotent... The Omniscience... The Omnipresent... No one in this universe has greater power or love than He... Thank You Father for calling me & choosing me... I am nothing without You & everything with You... Use me to do Your Will that You maybe glorified magnificently and that others may share in Your Wonder & Awe...

Day 233: **Do not be afraid...**

Jeremiah **41, 42, 43, 44, 45**

This is the message from YHWH to His loyal ones..."Do not be afraid"... But to those who walk according to their own desires, serving their flesh rather than YHWH, "Be very afraid"... All that Jeremiah prophesied in those days stands today... However the last of the biblical prophets was our precious Saviour The Messiah... He left us The Way to follow... & That Way is Him... All that He did & all that He said is what He left as a legacy... an example for our walk... He was truly, explicitly, absolutely & ultimately obedient to the Father... & that's exactly how we need to be... following the word written in the Scriptures with love... praying always for wisdom, discernment, understanding & accurate knowledge of the Truth from our Father YHWH El Almighty via His Holy Spirit... Amen!

Day 234: **Israel will be saved...**

Jeremiah **46, 47, 48**

YHWH will destroy all nations who choose to serve their own false gods... however He will save Israel but not without punishment... & not all Israel... only those found with a good conscience towards YHWH... YHWH loves the world that is why He gave His only Son so those exercising faith in Him will not perish but have everlasting life... Everyone has a chance... everyone has a choice... the key is to make the Right One...

Day 235: Sabbath Sanctuary...

Jeremiah 49, 50

This is our day of rest... rest from a week of doing the Father's work... rest from the contending with trials & tribulations... rest from intrusive thoughts, distressing feelings, tiring actions... rest for 24 hours to spend in truly quality time with YHWH... retrospective of our week being self-reflective & self-aware... singing in joy... giving thanks for the protection & guidance from our Father... & rest to revitalise us for the coming week... The 7th Day is the Sabbath YHWH made for man... let us rejoice & be glad in it...

Day 236: Babylon's devastating end proclaimed…

Jeremiah 51, 52

YHWH pronounces the devastating end for Babylon through Jeremiah the Prophet… there is reference to the selling of merchandise, worshipping of carved images and deceiving the nation with false doctrines… Woe to those who have not listened to the Truth of YHWH but have instead chosen to continue following all the falseness of Babylon who represents all of today's major churches… YHWH's Chosen Race surely suffered as a result of their disobedience when they were given into the hands of the Babylonians… but YHWH did not allow the Babylonians to go unpunished for their wickedness against Zion…

Day 237: Perfection of beauty?

Lamentations 1, 2

Lamentations… wailing… grief… distress… This is not what YHWH intended for His Perfection of Beauty… But Israel, Jerusalem, Zion fell away from Him… He attempted everything to reconcile them… He sent prophets day & night then ultimately sent His Only Son… & still their ears & heart were hardened… What else could YHWH our Father do? His Son paid the ultimate price & it still wasn't' & isn't enough… Praise be to YHWH there is a remnant… Oh that I remain a part of it & become the Perfection of Beauty YHWH intends…

Day 238: Great is His Faithfulness...

Lamentations 3, 4, 5

Great is Your faithfulness... YHWH my Father... There is no shadow in turning with You... You change not... Your compassions they fail not... As You have been You forever will be... LAMENTATIONS 3:23... This is one of my favourite hymns taken from this Scripture... YHWH's faithfulness is indeed great... It is the greatest & it never fails... neither does His compassion... love... peace... & joy... All things good from the FATHER continue forever... to those who remain loyal & obedient to Him...

Day 239: Ezekiel the Prophet...

Ezekiel 1, 2, 3, 4

Another of YHWH's great prophets sent on great but strange missions... set tasks that nearly all of us would find very difficult to execute... These are truly courageous, chosen & very special men of YHWH... If these prophets were to perform these tasks today they would for sure be deemed mentally unwell & probably committed to mental health institutes... Is there an Ezekiel type brother or sister in your midst who has an odd, eccentricity about them & has been rebuked, ridiculed, scoffed, judged or derided at by those who do not understand them? Be careful because it is evident true men of YHWH manifest odd & eccentric behaviours... but you know them by their fruits... as long as they function on an intellectually & spiritually wise level doing good works for YHWH showing true compassion, love & the fruits of the Spirits then you know these are YHWH's...

Day 240: Tragedy for Israel...

Ezekiel 5, 6, 7, 8

What a terrible tragedy... YHWH is so merciful & knowing... It maybe a trivial thing to the nation the worshipping of false gods but it's an abomination to YHWH.... It's clear that the minds of those not for YHWH & following other gods is a mind warped & manipulated easily by the enemy... It is impossible to worship false gods & remain in union with YHWH's Holy Spirit... It is this Spirit that discerns between right & wrong... righteousness & iniquity... because this Spirit gives pure wisdom & accurate knowledge of YHWH... This is necessary for salvation because nothing toxic, evil, unrighteous can reside with the Father & the Son... Their very goodness naturally repels anything unholy & unclean... anyone clean knows YHWH therefore naturally only serves Him...

Day 241: Ezekiel pleads...

Ezekiel 9, 10, 11, 12

Ezekiel had first hand vision given to him by YHWH of the devastation to befall Jerusalem... It was evidently a distressing & traumatic image... so much so he pleaded for the remnant... & of course YHWH had promised He would save a chosen few... YHWH has His cherubs, angels, prophets & loyal ones all doing His will... He has & will allow all men to hear His truth first so His Righteousness is without question in the day of devastation...

Day 242: What YHWH says... YHWH does...

Ezekiel 13, 14, 15

How many times did YHWH speak? How many prophets did He have? How many times did He send them out to give His Word? Today He is still giving His Word... but who is truly listening? Who is fully understanding His Purpose for our lives? It is impossible for YHWH to lie because He is Holy & Righteous... therefore it is impossible for sin to dwell in Him... & this is what He wants for His People... But they have decided not to hear Him & have gone astray instead... Therefore only a remnant shall survive... those who hear YHWH's voice, listen & act accordingly...

Day 243: Holy Tree...

Ezekiel 16, 17

YHWH is the Vine Dresser... His Son is the Vine.... & we are the branches... Some are the original branches... & some have been grafted in... YHWH prunes the tree to rid it of rotten & dead branches to avoid contaminating or taking the source of life from the branches that are still alive... so that they can continue to flourish & bear beautiful fruits...

Day 244: YHWH's takes no pleasure in death…

Ezekiel 18, 19, 20

When I read the Scriptures of the Old Great Prophets it speaks so much of punishment & eternal destruction… It all sounds so awful… But it is clear & evident that YHWH our Father never ceased in trying to turn back Israel to Him… They were so stiff-necked, stubborn & stuck in their wicked, abominable ways… but oh my El… YHWH still loved them enough to send prophet after prophet to give them an exceedingly good chance for salvation… yet they still didn't listen… Instead they killed the prophets because they couldn't bear to hear the truth of their darkness or their unclean & wicked ways… He then sent His one & only precious Son… & yes… they didn't listen to Him either… & yes… they crucified Him for His Truth… & today is no different… YHWH is still giving everyone the chance of salvation… He does not have any pleasure at all that the wicked should die…

Day 245: Heart-breaking...

Ezekiel 21, 22

The devastation planned for the end times is indeed heart-breaking... but more so for Our Father who must be weeping terribly in His heart... How long His suffering must be... to watch His creation destroying themselves & others in the process generation after generation... Now is the time to seek our salvation whole heartedly... with fear & trembling... seeking it more than any other thing in this world for the Love of You Father & Your Son Yahsah Messiah...

Day 246: Women of YHWH...

Ezekiel 23, 24

Women of YHWH make Him proud... We have a specific role to play... Let us not do as Oholah & Oholibah did... Instead let us develop a beauty of the hidden person of the heart... an incorruptible beauty that is of a mild and quiet spirit... precious in the sight of YHWH (1 PETER 3)...

Day 247: YHWH's revenge...

Ezekiel 25, 26, 27

Do not avenge for yourself, says YHWH, but let vengeance be Mine... Though YHWH had warned His People that they would go into captivity because of their sins He did not accept the gloating & ill treatment from their enemies... Ammon, Moab, Philistia & Tyre... So He took vengeance on all of them on behalf of Judah & Jerusalem... These were cold, shameless, materialistic traders whose only concern was money, power, fame & fleshly desires... We live in a world saturated with people who believe in their selves as the power & have totally neglected or rejected The Creator... Instead they scoff & deride those who truly have the power... the Power of YHWH... Those who have come into true & total peace as well as the promise of eternal riches in glory... Only YHWH makes all things possible & with Him everything we do is successful... but only if it is in keeping with saving His Children... Our mission on this earth is to first be cleansed & be filled with His Holy Spirit... then used as His Holy Vessel to help heal & bring back His Children who are scattered throughout the 4 corners of the globe... Our society is consumed with believing that our business, our job, our education, our hobbies, our possessions are what make us who we are... but it isn't... What makes us who we are is YHWH El Almighty... All the things He enables is a means to an end to enable His Purpose to take place... So we must not get attached to these things and must allow YHWH to totally lead us… In this way we never get consumed with success, acknowledgement or fame… because YHWH will undoubtedly provides everything we need to succeed… What He wants should matter most… PSALMS 1… With man all things are not possible… but with YHWH our Father ALL things are possible… Any man ridiculing, deriding & attacking YHWH's Children because of who they are & what they are willing to do for Him YHWH will avenge… Amen!

Day 248: Tyre condemned...

Ezekiel 28, 29, 30

Satan... the destructor... King of Tyre... whose arrogance caused him to be permanently rejected & cast out from before YHWH is now an abomination causing destruction & death amongst the nation up to today... But his end is soon thank YHWH & our Messiah... Don't be fooled by those who say they come in the name of The Father... or those in high places who brag about who they are and what they have achieved... You will know them by their fruits... Not just some but all the fruits of a good tree are good... Let us be producers of good fruit and not chase after the things of this world... They are vanity & will be destroyed... Instead chase after the things of the Spirit...the things of YHWH... They are living & for eternity...

Day 249: Egypt's downfall… Ezekiel's Song…

Ezekiel 31, 32, 33

Egypt has taken a fall & will not come back up… Their arrogance & idolatrous worship has condemned them to the Pit… Ezekiel, the Watchman, gave the prophecy to YHWH's people as He had commanded but yet they did not listen… Today is no different… YHWH is raising Watchmen… If these Watchmen do not let those who are idolatrous worshippers, arrogant in their ways, making money & other materialistic things their priority, know that YHWH will forgive & forget all their sins if they turn to face Him, seek forgiveness & from then walk righteously in their ways, they will still be destroyed but the blood will be on the Watchmen's hands… But if the Watchmen make them aware of the impending doom & they adhere to YHWH's Words then all will be saved & live… The question is… Who are the Watchmen? & those who say they are… are they giving the accurate knowledge of The Word spoken by YHWH? You will know them by their fruits & their prophecies will come to pass…

Day 250: Morning Father...

Ezekiel 34, 35, 36

Good morning my Father... How are You this day? What can I do for You today? I am so fortunate to know You & to have You in my life... I know there is so much more for me to discover about You it overwhelms me with joy... I love You so much that my heart is filled with tears of gladness... You have truly made Yourself known to me that I fear You with reverence due totally to Love, Your Awe & Omnipotence... Oh how I wish the whole world would come to know You that we could all live in peace, love & true harmony... Let me be a pleasure to You today & always...

Day 251: Day of Reckoning...

Ezekiel 37, 38, 39

Ezekiel prophesied the end times... the renewing of YHWH's People & the destruction of the enemies... Revelation confirms this prophesy... YHWH's Righteousness & Holiness will be fully confirmed & completely reflective of every word spoken by Him... He cannot lie... It shall be done...

Day 252: YHWH's Temple...

Ezekiel 40, 41, 42

An Angel of bronze appeared with a measuring rod… 6 cubits (9ft) long… to measure the Temple of YHWH… "In My Father's House there are many mansions… If it were not so I would have told you…" — JOHN 14… The time of YHWH is approaching fast… The Messiah is preparing a place for us so where He is there we will be also… He says where He is we know & the Way we know also… Messiah is the Way, the Truth & the Life & none of us can come to His Father except through Him… He came to earth to exemplify the way we need to go… All we have to do is follow His Way… Simple… As the Father was in Him so The Messiah is in those sanctified by the Holy Spirit therefore walking according to His Way… Only those sanctified by the Holy Spirit receive the Truth because the Holy Spirit is Truth & is the Only One who knows the Truth of The Father & The Son…

Day 253: Be well with YHWH…

Ezekiel 43, 44, 45

All is well with YHWH when we walk according to His Ways… His Glory lights up the whole earth & His Voice resonates the sound of abundant waters… Who can truly know YHWH Almighty… The Most High El… Creator of the Universe other than His Son Yahsah The Messiah? Only those with the accurate knowledge of Truth…

Day 254: YHWH is There...

Ezekiel 46, 47, 48

The very last verse of the Book of Ezekiel... "YHWH Almighty is There"... That is the name of the City... & all the Gates surrounding it are named after all Twelve Tribes of Israel... Jacob's sons... Who wouldn't want to dwell amid that city? Father YHWH The Most High... You lead from the front & guide from behind... I am so grateful, thankful, blessed & amazed by Your Mercy, Wisdom, Loving Kindness & Security... I never want to be without You & I only want to live according to Your desires... I may have wants but if they do not fit in with Your plans for my life then do away with them my Father... I know without doubt that You will always take care of my needs & give me joy in abundance... I have already experienced these things & I know Your Promise will never fail... I love You Father deeper & deeper each moment & thank You for my Saviour & joint Heir the Messiah Yahsah... without whom I would never know You...

Day 255: Yahsah is coming…

Joel 1, 2, 3

What a fantastic chapter Joel 2 is… Yahsah is coming & that is a fact… He is coming to claim back His Lost Sheep… all those who call upon His Name… YHWH will restore the years that the locust has eaten… He will deal wondrously with us so we will never be put to shame again… Who really can refuse His Promise? Many many people will… but not me… I stand firmly in my faith on Your Word Father… Never may I stray for Your Spirit is already upon me & I am in love with You & Your Ways… I give praise & thanks to You alone for my salvation, my life & Your Son Yahsah the Messiah… the beautiful Redeemer who reconciled me to You… Amen!

Day 256: True Faith delivers...

Daniel 1, 2, 3

What an Almighty YHWH we serve... What an awesome yet fearful sight to see 3 of YHWH's children unhurt in a scorching furnace aided by His Angel... There is nothing impossible for the Creator to do... Daniel was given deep insight, wisdom & knowledge that belongs only to YHWH... so much so that the king promoted him to Prime Minister... Daniel, Hananiah, Mishael & Azariah were truly loyal men with absolute faith in YHWH... This faith was truly rewarded & delivered them from all harm... They were prepared to die for their El because their faith ensured them that they would see the face of YHWH & His Son... that a life with Them was worth more than any other... YHWH knows best...

Day 257: Daniel & Darius...

Daniel 4, 5, 6

How beautiful the faith of King Darius in YHWH El Almighty was even though he wrote a decree against anyone not serving his god... It was so evident that his faith in Daniel was a result of experiencing Daniel's power, light, wisdom & knowledge given from The Most High... He even fasted from food & sleep so that Daniel would be delivered from the mouth of the lions... So prayed so done... Absolutely moving & touching display of compassion & faith from Darius... He knew that the men who had commanded the decree were evil & punished them according to their wicked deeds... I feel such an overwhelming sense of emotion when I witness & experience such dedicated faith & compassion as Darius who openly appeared to serve another god but whose heart was evidently loving & connected to YHWH's Spirit...

Day 258: Shine the Light...

Daniel 7, 8, 9

I have come across many people in my daily walk of life who say they are with the Creator serving & worshipping Him... Most are church-goers... Catholics, Adventists, Baptists, Jehovah Witnesses... All believing they are saved & born again into the Holy Spirit... Then I hear their gossiping... their merciless judgements... their snipping & unconstructive criticism... their lack of compassion... their lack of forgiveness... their envy masked as anger... & it's clear they are not born again... They are not shining a Light for The Messiah... They are misled & mistaken... When did The Messiah ever display these negative traits? I weary & I sigh... then I remind myself that YHWH has called me just as He calls all His Children to go forth & bring His Children back to him to be cleansed... I am now reminded of GALATIANS 5:22-26 The fruit of the Spirit... This is the destined walk of YHWH's Children... Ambassadors of The Messiah to emulate these fruits... I know, for me to do the Will of the Father & still remain in their midst despite their negativity just to continue witnessing & guiding them to YHWH, if it were not for long-suffering & self-control I would be no use & no good to myself let alone anyone else... It is a long, difficult & lonely road at times but thank YHWH I am never alone & it is all worth it... To know I am not just saving my life but the lives of anyone else who wants to live in Yahsah... Those of my family, friends, colleagues, acquaintances & strangers... Anyone & everyone deserves a chance to be saved... Didn't YHWH create us all?

Day 259: How close is the end?

Daniel 10, 11, 12

What a blessing & an assurance to be in the Arms of YHWH… never having to worry about my destiny because I have made a vow to remain in the Law of my Father so my destiny is assured with Him… There is no safer place to be… here on this earth & in the Paradise Earth to come… I would rather serve my El & relinquish the things of this earth & live than to have all the empty treasures of this world & look forward to eternal damnation… because in the end what's the point of temporary, fleeting pleasure here when eternal pleasure with YHWH awaits us?

Day 260: YHWH is good...

Ezra 1, 2, 3

YHWH is good & His mercies endures forever... toward His Children... He doesn't know how to be anything else... He is responsible for creation & takes care of all our needs... Who is anyone to contend with Him? I know my place... & my place is in submission to my Father...why? Because as my Creator He knows me better than anyone else... better than I know myself... I know for sure YHWH is The Creator & all the days of my life He will always be my El... my Saviour... my Father...

Day 261: Temple rebuilt...

Ezra 4, 5, 6; Psalms 137

Our bodies are a temple & just like YHWH's Temple in Jerusalem our temple is being rebuilt... We have been broken, melted & are now going through remoulding... Unless we are 'rebuilt' in righteousness the Holy Spirit cannot dwell within us... He can guide & instruct us but to be born again we must first be cleansed & then the Father allows His Spirit to dwell within us... It is impossible for the Spirit to live within darkness & we all come to the Father with unrighteousness... We serve a loving & merciful El... He doesn't leave us alone... everything we need He supplies to those who prayer earnestly with a good conscience towards Him...

Day 262: The Chosen...

Haggai 1, 2

It is an honour & a blessing to be chosen by YHWH because you know you have been cleansed & filled by His Holy Spirit... You have full protection & eternal salvation because once you are chosen by the Most High you are truly born again & there is no going back... Once the Holy Spirit dwells in you your every step is guided & to step onto the wrong path would literally mean you have consciously decided to disobey the Spirit... that is considered blasphemy of the Spirit... the unforgivable sin... Let that never be the case...

Day 263: The Anointed...

Zechariah 1, 2, 3, 4

Zechariah is an intriguing book & feels different from other biblical books... There is clear reference of Satan taking his stand against YHWH's Anointed & being rebuked by The Most High... There is reference of Yahsah The Son of El as The Redeemer of YHWH's Children... There is reference of 2 very special Anointed of YHWH who stand beside The Father... & there is clear reference of The Angels referred to as 'Fathers'... The Father will always reveal His sacred secrets, His mysteries, & confidential matters to His Children... those who obey His Words with accurate knowledge of His Scriptures... His Anointed...

Day 264: How Great You are...

Zechariah 5, 6, 7, 8, 9

Oh YHWH my El when I'm in awesome wonder & consider all the works your hands have made... I see the stars & hear the mighty thunder... Your power throughout the universe is displayed... Then sings my soul YHWH El to me... How great You are...

Day 265: Doom... then Deliverance...

Zechariah 10, 11, 12, 13, 14

Only YHWH can truly save... through His Son Yahsah The Messiah... There is no escaping how awful that day will be... when the flesh of those who would not accept The Messiah as their Saviour & YHWH as the Most High El are dissolved... YHWH is truly merciful & His Arms are still opened wide... Now is the time to accept He is the Creator so all flesh can live while there is still a chance... All glory belongs to YHWH Almighty... I know that the time is near & I walk in faith with my Father... I choose deliverance over doom every time... I believe every Word of my El & know that there is no time or room for complacency... What is seen with fleshly eyes is minuscular in comparison to what those eyes don't see... YHWH reveals His secrets to His Obedient... those who love Him...

Day 266: Queen Esther...

Esther 1, 2, 3, 4, 5

Esther is one of my favourite books in the bible... She came from humble beginnings... an orphan raised by her loving uncle Mordecai, taken captive by Chaldeans then prepared and chosen as queen to replace a disobedient one... All the while, as with all YHWH's chosen who rise into huge societal positions, they are there for the purpose of delivering YHWH's children from the unforeseen harm... Mordecai remained still an overseer of his niece & continued to give her spiritual instruction... Esther as an obedient child took her commission wholeheartedly & was prepared to die to save her people if that's what it took... I have taken many 3 day fasts on account of reading Esther & on being led by the Holy Spirit...

Day 267: When YHWH is for you...

Esther 6, 7, 8, 8, 10

When YHWH is for you who can be against you? YHWH truly takes care of His Children... to those who obey Him... to those who stand firm in their faith... Esther & Mordecai were two such people... They relied on the faith they had in YHWH... They used the wisdom YHWH had given them & because of faith they exhibited humility & integrity... These qualities shine brightly to others... even to kings... & because of such, favour is granted more than one could ever imagine... So Esther is crowned queen & given leave to make petition to the king as much as half his kingdom (127 provinces)... & Mordecai was advanced into the 2nd highest position in the land... These are the great things YHWH does for His People... not for their glory but for His... Esther & Mordecai used their superior positions to help bring peace & goodness to their people... never self-seeking or boasting in themselves... They are two exemplary biblical figures of how standing in faith wins YHWH's favour, protection, wisdom, dignity & prosperity...

Day 268: Pagan sin...

Ezra 7, 8, 9, 10

Here we are again... Israel sinning yet again... playing the harlot with the Ammonites, Perizzites, Canaanites, Jebusites, Hittites, Moabites, Amorites & Egyptians... the first known Pagans... This was an abhorrence to Ezra... So much so when he heard he tore his clothes and ripped out the hairs from his head & beard... He wept bitterly & went into fasting & praying... His prayers were indeed answered & all of Israel accepted the commandment of YHWH by putting away their pagan wives & separating from their pagan children... turning back to their El clean & ready to serve Him... Most of these men were Levi priests... those who were the chosen inheritance of YHWH... those tasked with Spiritual leadership yet they were setting terrible examples & leading YHWH's children astray... What was happening then is still happening now... Listen & observe... seek out your own salvation with fear & trembling...

Day 269: Nehemiah... a faithful servant...

Nehemiah 1, 2, 3, 4, 5

The selfless acts of the true servants of YHWH are to be truly admired... I so aspire to doing the will of The Father... I know that it His will that I share the Good News of The Gospel... To help reconcile His Children to Him... To dedicate time in helping to heal His People... To encourage others in The Messiah through exemplary conduct... All this is only possible through my faith... This includes reading my Scriptures & meditating on them daily... Being a doer of the Word... Shining a Light for the Father by walking in obedience just as The Messiah did & portraying all the fruits of The Spirit which are... love, peace, joy, long-suffering, self-control, meekness, faithfulness & kindness... It is impossible to exhibit this with purity in our own strength... only YHWH Almighty can enable this in us through our desire & total obedience to Him... He gives us the Wisdom & accurate knowledge through His Holy Spirit... Through this process our minds become clearer... We are transformed by this renewing & do not conform to the things of this world... We can then hear the Voice of YHWH & His Angels clearly giving us instruction & guidance... Only then will we truly know who we are & our purpose in this life... & even if we are falling or fall He is always there to pick us up... We must strive for perfection even though we are not perfect... Our expectations of our walk with YHWH must be high... "Reach for the moon & even if you miss you will fall amongst the stars"... Reach to YHWH & you will dine with Him together with Yahsah His Son & His Saints & Angels...

Day 270: Hand of YHWH...

Nehemiah 6, 7

True faith means having no doubt that YHWH will deliver you from all harm... that anything you pray in His Name & the Name of His Son will be granted in accordance with His spiritual matters... This means letting go of the fleshly things as more important knowing He will always give us according to our needs... Our focus should be on spiritual matters to progress His Kingdom because in the end that's all that will remain & truly matters...

Day 271: YHWH's Covenant...

Nehemiah 8, 9, 10

Entering into a covenant with The Most High should not be done without serious thought... In order to walk according to YHWH's Law we need to know them... & the only way to know them is by reading & meditating on The Scriptures daily... People are either complacent, lazy or misled as to what is truly involved in gaining salvation... I know that even for me, a Child of YHWH, a Follower of The Messiah, I have difficulty daily... I identify my weaknesses & bring them to The Father... I do not hide them or fool myself into believing I am walking in total righteousness... This is truly the only way we can progress... It proves to The Father what kind of Follower I am... It shows true humility & a readiness to demonstrate this to all as an exemplary Child of The True El in order to empower, edify & encourage others... It really is about YHWH & His Son as the Most Important... because without Them we would be nothing, we are nothing & will be nothing... Just as The Messiah experienced it can be a lonely path but a truly rewarding & powerful one nevertheless... I have experienced loneliness outside of YHWH's Spirit & within it... The difference is even when I experience loneliness within YHWH's Spirit I know for sure I am not alone... The loneliness is a void, a darkness that the Enemy plants within my mind... a form of depression... It is also the ploy he machinates in others by planting deceptive thoughts in their minds... Only the accurate knowledge of The Most High can give the wisdom & discernment to understand these processes & respond in a righteous way... then in this way we preserve our salvation & joy as well as that of our fellow brethren...

Day 272: YHWH causes to become…

Nehemiah 11, 12, 13; Psalms 126

If it were not for YHWH none of us would exist… Mere man could not imagine the full extent of YHWH… Human thought is a minute percentage of YHWH's thoughts… They could never compare… Fleshly thought with limited constraints could never contend with the infinite Wisdom of the Spirit of YHWH… yet the arrogance of man always tries… & as always these attempts are futile but will indubitably lead to destruction… I look around & as much joy as I have in knowing my Beautiful Father YHWH Almighty & my Beautiful Redeemer The Messiah Yahsah, I unfortunately experience sadness & disappointment because of those who do not want to know Them… This fact cannot be ignored…

Day 273: The Sun of Righteousness...

Malachi 1, 2, 3, 4

I loved reading Malachi especially the Scripture referring to "The Sun of Righteousness arising with healing in His Wings"... This has been a favourite of mine since experiencing a sunrise on a plane to Spain... I still have the photo I took of it & use it with this particular verse in some of my marketing... The Messiah is The Sun... & for sure He has come with healing in His wings... I know because I am living proof of that healing... I love my Messiah... He gave Himself as a sacrifice for me... what a selfless, loving act... He is a sure example of how we have to be if we want to reside in the mansion He is preparing for us... I realise today that one thing we do as humans that is killing us is our negative judgement of others... I had a beautiful fellowship with a very dear Sister in The Messiah & following this The Spirit revealed that when we judge others it prevents us getting close to them & if we are not close how can we show The Messiah's love... How can we encourage others (family, friends, colleagues, strangers) to accept His Walk if we are not walking like Him? YHWH requires mercy & that means learning to accept no one is perfect... All have sinned (including me) & fall short of the glory of YHWH... Let us stop casting judgement & instead let us develop mercy, understanding & unconditional love...

Day 274: Yahsah The Messiah... The Son of YHWH...

Luke 1; John 1

It's the 1st day of October & I am so excited to have read the 1st account of Messiah entering into this world... & about the Prophet John the Baptist... The Messiah the Only begotten Son of YHWH whom The Father has given the throne of King David... whose Kingdom is forever... I love reading from the beginning of The Messiah's ministry... It is so uplifting, enriching, empowering & energising... It has been a revelation reading from Genesis to Luke... I now have a fuller understanding of why The Messiah came into the world... Many churches have made the world believe He came for those outside of the Church... but that is not entirely true... He came for those from the House of Jacob... those who have sinned & turned away from YHWH's Commandments... John the Baptist, the son of Zachariah, a Levitical priest, came to prepare His Way... to bear witness of Him as The Messiah... Today nothing has changed... The churches are still in a poor state with its false doctrines & abominations... congregation members need to beware & search for the Truth...

Day 275: The True Name of The Messiah is Yahsah...

Matthew 1; Luke 2

A few years ago the True Name of The Messiah was revealed to me... It has long since been established that Jesus is not the original name of the Son of YHWH... Jesus has been explained by many scholars & wordsmiths to be a 'transliteration' of the Son of El's Hebrew Name... Many say it's Yeshua but the True Name & pronunciation is YAHSAH... YHWH is the Tetragrammaton found in original Scriptural texts & is the True Hebrew Name of The Father... It was removed centuries ago from the bible & replaced with 'LORD' written all in uppercase... YHWH comes from the Hebrew verb 'hawah' meaning 'to become' or 'come into existence'... YHWH means 'HE causes to become or come into existence'... YAHSAH is derived from His Father's Name and means 'YAH is salvation'... MATTHEW 1:21 reveals this: "...& she will bring forth a Son & you shall call His Name [Yahsah] for He will save His

People from their sins"... We know for a fact that Angel Gabriel did not tell Mary to call Him 'Jesus' as that name did NOT EVEN exist in that time... We also know from this verse in MATTHEW that Messiah had a name that meant He will save His People from sins... All this is relevant, just as His Name Immanuel means "with us is El" (MATTHEW 1:23)... Luke 2:21 states "...His name was called 'Jesus', the name given by the angel before He was conceived"... Again we know for a fact that the angel did not give the name 'Jesus'... so if this was not the name given what was? "A good name is better than precious ointment... & the day of death better than the day of one's birth" — PROVERBS 7:1... This is no more relevant to anyone else than The Messiah Himself... BUT hey... don't just take my word for it... search for yourself... "Seek & you will find..." — MATTHEW 7:7...

Day 276: Refuge for The Messiah... The Messiah a Refuge...

Matthew 2

The destiny of The Messiah was determined before the foundations of the earth... Joseph a loyal servant of YHWH & earthly father to The Messiah could hear the angels speak... He listened & obeyed... for if he didn't The Messiah would not have been our Saviour... Egypt played the role of refuge for The Son of YHWH & His parents... & today The Messiah is our Refuge as He also was then for the salvation of all those calling upon the name of Yahsah... He had His own star that led wise men to give homage to Him & bear gifts of gold, frankincense & myrrh... What do these symbolise? I believe they are symbolic of refinement, sweet aromatic prayer & death...

Day 277: Sons of YHWH...

Matthew 3; Mark 1; Luke 3

From Abraham to Messiah was 42 generations... 14 from Abraham to David... 14 from David to Israel's captivity in Babylon... 14 from Jeconiah to Joseph, the earthly father of The Messiah... But from Adam to Abraham there was another 20 generations... Adam being the first man, the son of YHWH...

Day 278: The tempter...

Matthew 4; Luke 4, 5

Imagine that Yahsah The Messiah is the Son of The Most High... yet even He the devil tried to tempt... So if He being the Son of YHWH was tempted how much more us... It is imperative we are reading & living by the Words of Scriptures... This is all the tempter used to try & make Yahsah fall whilst in His weakest state having just completed a 40-day fast... But Yahsah knew the Scriptures, the Word of YHWH as these were written by His Anointed by the authority of The Father's Holy Spirit... "Reading Scriptures a day keeps the tempter away"...

Day 279: The Father & The Son...

John 2, 3, 4

JOHN 3:16 states, "YHWH so loved the world He gave His Only Begotten Son... that everyone exercising faith in Him should not perish but possess everlasting life" JOHN 3:35 states... "The Father loves The Son..." I remember when I first started to doubt the trinity... & it was no wonder... But my pastor kept trying to make me believe that YHWH The Father was The Messiah Who came down to earth in the flesh... & when his explanations still didn't make sense he would then say... "It's a mystery"... What a ludicrous doctrine... JOHN clearly states a distinction between The Father & The Son... It is a serious misconception to believe in the trinitarian doctrine... JOHN 3:33 states, "He who has received His testimony has certified that YHWH is true"... YHWH reveals all His Sacred Secrets & mysteries to His Children... why would He want to hide them? MARK 4:11 states... "To you it has been given to know the mystery of The Kingdom of YHWH... but to those on the outside everything is in parables unless they should turn back & their sins be forgiven"... YHWH Almighty has no hidden secrets from His Children... He is The Father & Yahsah The Messiah is His Son... We follow The Messiah as an example of true obedience... that was why He came down to earth...

Day 280: The Sabbath...

Matthew 8; Mark 2

The Sabbath is such a blessed day... a true gift from YHWH... It's a day to rest from the work of the week... not just physical work but more specifically Spiritual work... For those who are evangelising, ministering, teaching, prophesying, healing in the name of YHWH throughout the week The Sabbath is a very important time to take for rest... The tempter hates those doing the Will of YHWH so he is roaming around seeking whoever he can devour... He plays with the mind by creating machinations... taunting, ridiculing, mocking, deriding, accusing, deceiving... He does this through any means possible... using anyone he can... colleagues, friends, family, strangers... This psychological & emotional attack takes its toll even when we are aware & rely on YHWH for the wisdom, knowledge & discernment to respond righteously... The Sabbath gives us the time to revitalise & reenergise for the week to come by spending it in The Spirit of YHWH... We are then given everything we need to strengthen us for the week to come so we can continue on our path of salvation encouraging & leading as many people as we can on the path of salvation also... Amen to our Father of The Sabbath The Messiah Yahsah...

Day 281: The Walk with The Messiah...

John 5

I love reading the Gospel of John... it's one of my favourite books in the bible if not the favourite... It speaks so clearly about Yahsah's life & His purpose here on Earth... He came to exemplify The Way for all of YHWH's Children... He speaks so eloquently of His relationship with His Father & emulates the accuracy of true obedience to The Most High... The Messiah is so beautiful... It is indeed a difficult journey walking in His Footsteps... He knows it & so does His Father... Here shows their beauty in love & mercy... Had The Messiah not have come down in the flesh living in the flesh as we do He could not advocate for us so explicitly... He empathises, He mediates, He forgives & He delivers us... Their love truly abounds...

Day 282: Accurate knowledge...

Matthew 12; Mark 3; Luke 6

I am so excited having reached the Gospels in my plan of reading the bible in one year... It has been such a revelation reading from the Old Testament through to the New... I would never come to realise the true understanding of why The Messiah came to Earth... My heart is filled with joy & gladness reading about the life & works of my beautiful Saviour... I also feel grief & sadness at the awful treatment He endured... I know He has come through the pains of the flesh but He still has His Followers out here who are going through tribulations & continuing to suffer pain... He Himself & His Father are also suffering as a result... It is so important to live good through the strength of The Almighty... We can only know how to truly live good according to The Holy Commandments of YHWH through reading our Scriptures daily & meditating on them... It is so easy for the enemy to mislead us if we don't... YAHSAH tells us that... "Everyone who is PERFECTLY trained will be like His Teacher"... Let us all who say they love The Father & The Son enter into our Perfect Training... Let us make a difference in this world & be true pleasures to Our Saviours...

Day 283: Light of the World...

Matthew 5, 6, 7

I could easily have highlighted the whole of the 3 chapters of Yahsah's Sermon on the Mount (MATTHEW 5-7) as every verse is so relevant, integral, enlightening, true, edifying & wonderful... You can imagine how eloquently Yahsah spoke & how amazing it would have been to be in His presence as He presented these Laws in the mountains... But imagine there were those there that did not accept Him or His Words... They actually hated Him enough to kill Him for the very truth in the Words He spoke... Let us shine our light as our Messiah did... Unless we are in Scriptures we will never know how we should be... we will never be cleansed... & our salvation will be far from us... Let us shine our light for the Glory of YHWH our Father just as The Messiah did so obediently & passionately...

Day 284: Labour for YHWH...

Matthew 9; Luke 7

Yahsah The Messiah knows His Children & so knows their needs... There are enough of His Children out there who are searching for the truth coming to the 'churches' of this world & struggling to find it... So they become scattered... They are lost & seeking their salvation... YHWH is raising labourers to go out to gather His Children & to bring them back to Him... I thank YHWH that I have been called in that number having a desire in my heart to serve Him... making myself available & being made able to do HIs Will... "The harvest is truly plentiful... but unfortunately the labourers are few... therefore let us pray to YHWH to be sent out as labourers in the field to collect the harvest" — MATTHEW 9:37, 38... Know The Truth to share The Truth thereby becoming a perfect labourer for YHWH through His First Fruit of Creation... our Saviour YAHSAH The Messiah... Amen!

Day 285: Know YHWH… know The Messiah…

Matthew 11

To know The Messiah is to know The Father… & to know The Father is to know The Messiah… The Messiah revealed the Father to His disciples whilst He was here on earth… Now He is sitting on the right hand side of The Father in Heaven He reveals Him to us through The Holy Spirit… through His exemplary obedience to YHWH's Commandments & our obedience to Him through our adherence to The Word of Scriptures…

Day 286: The Gift of YHWH...

Luke 11

I am so in awe of My Father & so grateful to My Saviour... I look at where I am today in my faith & marvel at how much YHWH My El has opened my eyes... Things I could only hope to know years ago are being revealed to me now... I know I am in the bosom of My Father... "The effective & fervent prayer of a righteous man avails much" JAMES 5:16... What we ask for is crucial... I want to be Holy pleasing to YHWH... to be a powerful woman of ministry... to be a shining light to the nation... to have longevity of life, prosperity in all things, humility, peace, joy, endurance & all the love my YHWH can give me so that I may bring as many of My Father's lost sheep back to Him... My prayer is simply to receive His Holy Spirit so that in all I think, feel, say or do is totally by His Guidance & not mine...

Day 287: The Parables of The Messiah...

Matthew 13; Luke 8

I felt sadness reading today's scriptures from my yearly plan... Imagine having the beautiful Messiah in your midst... His only objective is to heal the sick & disabled, forgive sinners, give life to those who are dead in spirit so the Children of YHWH can return to Him... He goes out to do just this amid towns, villages, cities (even His own locality) but because The Power of His Marvellous Works are so awesome & great fear falls upon the masses... so instead of embracing Him they reject Him... What fools they were... & still are today... There are so many people singing out the praises of The Father but how many are really true to Him & The Messiah? He gave an accounting of the sower in a parable which His Disciples questioned... They were privileged to The Sacred Secrets... The Mysteries of Heaven... This privilege has also been given to all those who believe in the True Name of The Messiah... He is Salvation & He reveals all understanding to those who know Him & live according to the Commandments He was given by His Father & exemplified whilst He lived in the flesh... He is The Sower whose desire is to plant seeds in the good heart of man... on good soil... but which substance do you represent? The wayside... the stony places.... the thorny bush? I thank YHWH & my Beloved Messiah that His Seed has definitely fallen on the good soil that only He could have prepared for me... I have experienced riches of this world... I have experienced trials & tribulations... I have come to understand the True doctrines of The Messiah... & I am still standing strong in the love of my Saviour & my El YHWH The Most High... I will not be trampled, eaten, choked or scorched by the enemy & the things of this world by the Grace of The Almighty... because at the end of it all the things of this world are vanity & grasping for the wind (PROVERBS 2)... none of it matters... none of it will remain... only The things of The Father & The Son will remain eternally... in a Paradise Kingdom that our imagination could never comprehend but only the Holy Spirit can give us privilege to know...

Day 288: The Sower...

Mark 4, 5

I love the parable of The Sower & having read it 4 times in the last week as part of my bible reading plan I have been given such amazing insight into its meaning… more understanding that adds relativity to this enhanced interpretation… What this parable is highlighting is that are 4 types of 'Christians'… I use Christians for reference here as it is a title I no longer associate myself with… I am a Follower of The Messiah… A Messianite… So The Messiah is denoting 4 types of 'Followers'… Having meditated on these Words reflecting & introspecting I now see clearly the message The Messiah was giving His Disciples through this parable… This is a foundational message & talks about the beginning of YHWH's Kingdom… He creates a beautiful world & sows His Seed upon it… But all is not what He had hoped for & 4 different crops are produced… There are many in the world hearing about The Gospel of The Messiah… The Commandments of YHWH… but lacking understanding & wisdom because of complacency, inaccurate teachings, false doctrines, arrogance, foolishness, lack of insight & neglecting reading Scriptures… all this allows the Words they do have to be taken from them… Then there are those who hear The Word in a big social gathering, church, fellowship or group & the atmosphere is charismatic… singing, clapping, eating, drinking, laughing… The gathering gives a sense of belonging & identity… It's inviting & not reproving… but it's not rooted & other things in life take over… boyfriend, hobbies, laziness, nights out on the town & soon they've turned their backs & the Word is no longer in them… It has withered & died… Then there are those who hear the Word & comply with the 'rituals' of their faith… but the things of the world is where their heart is & takes precedence… expensive clothes, flashy cars, expensive holidays, high class living, superior status & positions in the secular things… so the Word is over shadowed by these desires and never comes to fruition… All of these are misled & in error… Then there are those who hear the Word & it rests in their hearts… They seek to find understanding & start to do the things according to the Word… They become conscience in their thoughts, words & deeds… They are in their Scriptures daily & benefit from being cleansed & healed by YHWH… They become filled with The Holy Spirit & share this Wonderful Wisdom with everyone shining The Light from the top of the Lamp Stand… Everything they do is a success because it is in complete accordance with The Father… from a good conscience & obedience… in truly knowing Him & The Son…

Day 289: The 12 Disciples...

Matthew 10

I know I will continue reading Scriptures for the rest of my life as long as YHWH makes it available to me... & as long as I do I know I will always be given new insight & revelations... This time round reading the bible from the beginning I have fully understood the links between all the books... When the original Scriptures were written they were not numbered in verses or chapters or split into new & old testaments... It was written chronologically depicting YHWH's blessings & promises & man's constant disobedience... The ultimate aim of The Scriptures is to give all YHWH's creation an opportunity to be saved... He wants to reconcile His Children through their obedience... He sent prophets... they did not obey them & perished... He sent His Son... they did not obey Him & are still perishing... The Messiah was given 12 disciples by His Father & these were chosen specifically to bring back 'The Lost Sheep'... those whose forefathers disobeyed The Law of YHWH & were then scattered... Because they were the chosen & rejected the first prize of YHWH He opened up the gift of salvation to all mankind that they may have a sharing of the prize... these are the Gentiles...

Day 290: YHWH's Beloved Son...

Matthew 14; Mark 6; Luke 9

The Messiah took a journey no man could endure... & He did it purely for love... Like Father... like Son... Their aim to bring back the Lost Sheep of Israel into their Righteous Inheritance... Such love They have for all mankind that YHWH opened the Promise to all... "Hear My Beloved Son"...

Day 291: Everlasting Saviour...

John 6

Many people who say they believe in YHWH make an initial decision to learn more about The Messiah then take their time to make a commitment to follow Him… I spent time reflecting on this yesterday evening after encouraging a close friend to read her scriptures daily as she had not been in the habit of doing so… She has just started fellowshipping again but says she is not ready to commit her life to The Messiah… I asked her what is stopping her & she was unable to find an answer… I spent time meditating on this with my Father & reading my daily scriptures I revisited JOHN 6:44… There lies the beauty of my Father… as always true to His Word… Anything we pray for in His Name shall be given… It was revealed to me that we in fact do not choose The Messiah… His Father calls us… We then make the decision to get know The Father through prayer, the reading of the Word & meditation… Then in this process through the connection of The Spirit we come to truly know The Father & The Son… It is this that enables our decision to make a commitment to walk with Messiah… cause once you know Them why would you choose to be a part of the world rather than being part of Them?

Day 292: Love... Light... Life...

Matthew 15; Mark 7

I am grateful for the life I have in The Messiah... What a privilege & an assurance to walk in the Love, The Light & The Life that is The Messiah... Dedicating my life to Him is the best decision I have ever made... I am free from the burdens of this flesh & the burdens of this world because all that matters is The Messiah & His Father... I stand firm in my faith... I have no doubt that what They promise They will deliver... anything I ask in Their Names I shall receive... MATTHEW 7:7... Amen!

Day 293: Lose to save…

Matthew 16; Mark 8

There is no doubt that many who have chosen to walk with The Messiah have not come to understand what that walk involves… I remember the year I was actually called… 2001… I would never have envisaged how much my life would change literally by the transforming of my mind… Everything I was before really depended on my fleshly thoughts… in other words all that I knew then… Now everything is dependent on what I know now & that is truly the thoughts of The Spirit… I share The Spirit of YHWH without doubt & have a desire to walk the difficult & narrow path of The Messiah… It truly means making a choice to deny the things of the flesh, the worldly things in order to do the Will of The Father… & that is enhancing His Kingdom by ministering His Word in the places that He wants to send me… Only The Holy Spirit can guide me if I am to survive psychologically, emotionally & most importantly spiritually… In my own strength my flesh would interfere giving the enemy an opportunity to manipulate… We can only come to this place when we dedicate to reading, meditating & acting on Scriptures daily… when we experience solitude & YHWH brings us to that place where we can survive alone relying totally on Him & His Son… when we make the decision to deny the things of this world to walk according to His Will which His Holy Spirit instructs… Yes we need to be self-sufficient so our Father will use the gifts He has given us that are based on our desires to understand ourselves & others so we can make a living... thereby putting the financial resources earnt into building & maintaining 'His Church'... Our only purpose on this world as Followers of The Messiah & Children of YHWH is to reconcile ourselves to The Father & help to bring His Lost Sheep back to His Fold... It is not about gaining worldly status by making monetary profit so we can look good or feel good as those in the world do... Yes we are a Royal Priesthood therefore we have majestic status... He will always take care of us but we must be willing to live a humble existence as Kings & Queens using our prominence predominantly for our Father & Saviours sake...

Day 294: Prayer & fasting...

Matthew 17; Mark 9

I've truly come to know how important prayer & fasting is... & knowing this I pray several times in the day when needed & I fast regularly... now at least once a week for 24 hours & 3-day fasts when a serious matter is at hand or in preparation to do a work for YHWH... Practising abstinence forces me to focus on The Father... without whom I could never get through the long fasts especially... Fasting helps to understanding compulsions and impulse control... It increases spiritual connection to The Father especially when the fast has been initiated & guided by the Holy Spirit... Regular fasting increases the Power of the Spirit & the mind therefore revealing more & more of YHWH's Sacred Secrets & Mysteries...

Day 295: Forgiveness...

Matthew 18

Psalms 130:3,4 is one of the most powerful verses in Scriptures... "If errors are what you count Oh YHWH who could stand... but there is true forgiveness with You in order that You maybe feared"... Reverent fear is not anxiety or dread... It is respect & awe... When I came to understand this scripture it took my breath away... It was a time when I had felt a deep desire to know YHWH & walk with loyalty & truth according to His Way... I needed to feel clean & the day I read this scripture I finally knew I was with my Father & my Saviour... There is true forgiveness with YHWH when we are fully contrite & sincere... Only the enemy brings to remembrance our past sins that YHWH has forgiven... This alerts us to the fact his dark spirit is present especially in the person recalling the past... Prayer is needed immediately in this situation so it doesn't escalate & glory remains with YHWH through our righteous conduct... Experiencing forgiveness in this way through YHWH has truly made me even more forgiving of others... It has such a wonderful impact on my relationships... It empowers me as I shine The Light for The Messiah & empowers others to want to get to know That Light...

Day 296: Signs of The Messiah...

John 7, 8

What more do people want in order to believe The Messiah is real? Not even His own brothers, those who claimed to be of YHWH, and those in the very presence of Him even believed He was The Messiah... Only those truly in the Spirit know The Son of YHWH... My heart weeps when I read about my Saviours plights amongst those who He came to save... They treated Him contemptuously... He must have been overwhelmingly disheartened... They truly were fools & lovers of the enemy... The Messiah knew this & they hated Him for it... He knew they were wolves in sheep's clothing...

Day 297: Yahsah's Flock...

John 9, 10

The Gospel of JOHN is one of the most powerful books in the bible... It clearly depicts Yahsah's mission... What is also elucidating is the explicit revelation of Him & His Father as separate beings... If one believes that they are one embodiment... The Messiah being The Father on Earth... then it means one neither knows The Father nor The Son... If one did they would know they are distinct... that The Messiah was sent on earth by His Father to do His Will... to save the Lost Sheep of Israel & other Sheep not from this Flock... Keep reading The Word praying to The Messiah & He will request from Our Father guidance & interpretation through The Holy Spirit...

Day 298: Rejoice... rejoice... Emmanuel...

Luke 10

I am rejoicing in the Spirit of YHWH... In my Saviour Yahsah for laying down His Life for me & the entire human race... & for my Father in Heaven for loving me & the whole world so much that He gave us His Son so we may live with Them in peace & true love for eternity... I'm in awe of my Saviours... I am so glad I was called & have been chosen to do a work for my Father... I rejoice in knowing I will reside with Them in Heaven in Their Glory, Power & Love... Amen!

Day 299: YHWH's Good Pleasure...

Luke 12, 13

It is the pleasure of our Father, The Most High, to give us His Kingdom... Imagine that... His pleasure... The Omnipotence, The Omniscience, The Omnipresence, The Awesome takes His pleasure in giving us His Glorious Kingdom... one which offers every kind of richness imaginable & unimaginable to man... not for the sake of status, greed or fleshly power... but for the sake of justice, mercy, peace, righteousness & love... Strive therefore to enter through the narrow gate which gives us entry to His Glorious Kingdom... for many will want to enter BUT will not be able to...

Day 300: The prodigal returns...

Luke 14, 15

I had forgotten how touching the parable of The Lost Son is... & probably because it has more resonance now than it did in my past... I am reflecting on my life but presently more on the life of my children... YHWH Almighty is truly my Father... & reading this parable today made me truly realised how much pleasure it gave Him when I returned to Him albeit not even realising I was one of His Children that had been scattered & left Him... I feel so moved by His love for me & by the commitment of His Son to give His Life so that not only I can live in Paradise with Them but my own children too... the one's He gave me to steward... my lovely people... How precious my children are & how precious I am to my Father & Messiah... Thank You Father for never forsaking me & for lifting me up every time I fell... Let me always be a pleasure to You...

Day 301: The Kingdom of YHWH...

Luke 16, 17

"Repent for the Kingdom of YHWH is near"... Yahsah made it clear that The Kingdom of YHWH cannot be seen but rather it is a state of heart... I know there are many who believe in The Messiah & The Father... They pray, they fellowship & show a modicum of faith... But when it really comes down to it those with wealth or a desire for the things of this world still chase after them not understanding that this behaviour is fleshly & no part of The Messiah or The Father... They will fool themselves into believing they are dedicated to their faith... that they are "in this world but no part of it"... Rubbish... Money, materialism, abundance of wealth is every bit a part of this world especially when importance is giving to it... so much so it causes conflict, stress & sin... We must be prepared to lose it all to gain life otherwise we will never be able to serve our Father whole-heartedly... & therefore gain all Their Wisdom & full gift of The Holy Spirit... which is what we need to enter into The Kingdom...

Day 302: The Saviour of the World...

John 11

It is evident that those who challenged The Messiah did not know He was The Messiah... otherwise would they have dared to crucify Him... Caiaphas the High Priest at the time prophesied that The Messiah was to die for the nation... one man sacrificed to save the whole world... The Jews made a plot from that day to put Him to death... I can assure you not because they believed they were fulfilling the Scriptures but to hold onto their status... they were more concerned about the things of the flesh than the things of the Spirit... They had no remorse or compassion for This Man who spoke nothing but truth... They had no shame, guilt or a contrite heart... They were willing to kill a man even one who had done no wrong... YHWH knew the heart of these greedy, egotistical, evil men & knew that they were capable of doing anything hence The Scriptures was able to be fulfilled because He knew these men would stoop to the ultimate low to hold onto the vanities of this world... MURDER... Unfortunately this crime still continues today but we have a Saviour who gives life to all those who believe in Him... those who exercise faith in Him... Amen!

Day 303: Dedication to The Messiah...

Luke 18

I have truly come to realise true dedication to The Messiah is a path that at times can be difficult, lonely, disheartening & tormenting... but that is only because the enemy tries all he can to attack me through my mind & the mind of others to take me away from my faith... My Father allows this because through every attempt I learn something new to strengthen my spiritual character & enhance my faith... YHWH Almighty... my Father... Father of my Living Saviour Yahsah The Messiah... He promises that all those who have left everything to do His Will... parents, siblings, children, partner, home... will receive much much more not just in eternity but in this present time... & my Father YHWH stands by every promise He makes... How wonderful it is for me to know Him... to finally come to a state of rest & peace in Him who is Real & True & The Most Potent... The Only Omnipotent... I have very little in terms of material wealth yet I have everything because of my Father & Messiah... Everything that makes all the difference... Everything that means anything & actually matters... Halleluyah & Amen!!!

Day 304: The Servant is Greatest...

Matthew 19; Mark 10

Imagine the 2nd most powerful being in this universe after His Father The Most High, Yahsah laid His life solely, explicitly & ultimately just to serve us... If that is not the epitome of true humility then what is? The Messiah really did come to show us the Way to be... All we need to do is read His Words & follow them with no doubt, no self-seeking or fleshly motives but with true love in our hearts to be reconciled back into YHWH's Fold... We need to all be servants of The Messiah letting go of the riches of this world to gain everything that the riches of Heaven will give for eternity... I know what I would rather have...

Day 305: Prayers are answered...

Matthew 20, 21

What an assured blessing & protection we have when we fully commit our lives to Yahsah... Anything we pray in the Name of YHWH we have been promised by The Messiah that we shall receive it... & He never lies... True faith will never doubt this... I love that I have this faith... It is comforting & peaceful... a life without anxiety... No one else can offer us this other than The Father... Our obedience to His Son & the love we have for Them Both as well as for His Creation assures us that all our prayers are heard... because those who are walking according to The Way will pray for those things pleasing to YHWH & not the flesh...

Day 306: All to YHWH's…

Luke 19

The Power is in YHWH & those YHWH has chosen to give it to… Those who have much more will be given… & those who have none even the little they have will be taken & given to those with much… There is no contending with The Father… The Glory is His & His Son's… so much so if we didn't give glory to Him stones themselves would… YHWH You are the Power & The Glory… Your Son is Your Love & Wisdom…

Day 307: Glory belongs to YHWH...

Mark 11; John 12

Yahsah Himself said... "Father glorify Your Name"... YHWH causes to become... Anyone operating in their own strength for their own gain will reap nothing in end times because they have not invested in the things pertaining to YHWH's eternal Spirit... "He who loves his life will lose it... but he who hates his life in this world will keep it for eternity"... Using your strength to do the things you believe you should do in this life amounts to fatigue, stress & vanity in the end... We were taught to believe this is the way it should be... It has been revealed that this isn't the way... well it's not the way for YHWH's Children... We know that the fleshly things are an enmity to YHWH... These are the things that make people 'love their life'... When a true Child of YHWH finally comes to know Him they finally realise that the fleshly things of this world do not matter & yearn to live according to The Spirit... This fleshly life then becomes burdensome & the desire & love for it disintegrates... so what is left is a hunger & desire to no longer be doing the things expected by the world & for the world but living for YHWH having Him as the absolute power source so we are no longer doing anything in our own strength... all the fatigue, stress & anxiety goes & what remains is peace, relaxation & joy... for eternity...

Day 308: The Greatest Commandment...

Matthew 22; Mark 12

This is the most important Scripture of the entire bible... "Love YHWH Almighty with all your heart, soul, mind & strength... then love your neighbour as you love yourself"... But in order to love even our Father & your neighbour we need to know how to love ourselves... What does that mean? We can only know love when we know YHWH... "Everyone who loves is born of YHWH & knows YHWH" 1JOHN 4:7... 1 CORINTHIANS 13 is the only chapter in the bible that gives a clear & definitive description of love... This is love perfected & the love we need for YHWH, for others & for ourselves...

Day 309: Teaching Truth...

Matthew 23; Luke 20, 21

Yahsah exemplified everything we as YHWH's Children need in our walk of faith... The Truth is the most important thing we need to have in order to impart everlasting life... There are many going out into the world ministering, evangelising, preaching & teaching who do not have the accurate knowledge of Truth... It is good to encourage others to come to The Messiah & in their faith by sharing our testimonies & witnessing... but unless we have accurate knowledge of Scriptures it is integral to refrain from giving the Word in ministry, to teach or to preach... Many like this are affiliated to churches therefore adhere to the doctrines of men & show partiality to 'their' churches... But The Messiah didn't... He did not belong to any religion or denomination... He just led in The Way... The Way of YHWH... I pray every day for The Truth & search for the things of YHWH... I do not leave my life in the hands of others... I listen & I observe... I eat my daily portion of spiritual food & I rely solely on The Holy Spirit... The Spirit of Truth...

Day 310: Only YHWH knows...

Mark 13

What an absolutely clear indication of YHWH Almighty...The Most High being The Greatest... above The Messiah & all the angels... The Messiah clearly states in MARK 13:32 that no one knows the day or hour when He shall appear in the 2nd Coming... not the Angels nor The Son... but only The Father... This is also indubitable evidence that the trinity is a false doctrine because if The Messiah, The Holy Spirit & YHWH The Father were one then The Messiah would know the hour & day of His Coming... When we are in direct communication with The True El of the universe abiding by The Word we will come to know The Truth & The Truth will set us free (JOHN 8:31,32)...

Day 311: Faithful Servants...

Matthew 24

When Yahsah comes will He really find faith on the Earth (LUKE 18:8)? How faithful are we as Followers of The Messiah? Do we work towards the things of the Spirit or do we have our feet still in the world hankering for the things of the flesh? Are we becoming complacent waiting for our Master without long-suffering neglecting the things pleasing to The Father by feeding our egos? Every day I am in meditation with my Father reflecting on my day with Him & introspecting on my conduct in my walk of faith... A daily devotion of this process is absolutely necessary in order to enhance our spirit, grow evermore closer to YHWH & His Son & to know the right things to do... If we are still hankering after the things of this world which are burdensome then the yoke which is carried is heavy, tormenting & consuming... therefore preventing the required peace & rest necessary for The Holy Spirit to operate within us... YHWH our El instructs us to seek Him first then His Righteousness & ALL other things will be given to us... Keep in your Faith... make sure that you are the 'good soil' that His Seed has fallen on so that when times are tough you remain standing firm in your faith... that you are a 'Faithful Servant'... & that Yahsah The Messiah indeed will really find faith on this Earth...

Day 312: Abundant Blessings...

Matthew 25

Doing the work of The Father is a pleasure… I once used to feel loaded & probably because I was doing the work others were setting for me to do… but I entered into a lone spiritual journey & truly found my Father… My relationship with Him has grown & the work I do for Him now is the work He has set for me to do… I yearn & desire to be that faithful servant… & what a joy & blessing it is to be… I am truly experiencing it in abundance… It is a pleasure, an honour & a privilege to serve You my Father & to follow in the Way of Your Son my Messiah Yahsah… My love to You Both… May you always experience pleasure, love & blessings from me & all Your Children… & long may I continue in my desire to serve You… Amen!

Day 313: But the flesh is weak…

Matthew 26; Mark 14

Those of us who have made a commitment to The Father by walking in The Ways of The Messiah must be diligent to be watchful & pray… Our Spirits are indeed willing but unfortunately our flesh is weak… We do the things pleasing to YHWH but we at times give into to the things of the flesh especially when we are tired or ladened because of the Spiritual work we do… But thank YHWH He is merciful, loving & forgiving… Never-the-less let us not take His beauty for granted but instead strive for perfection…

Day 314: Denial may come...

Luke 22; John 13

These Scriptures are one of the most sorrowful in the bible... Peter is devastated when he realises he denies his Messiah... & that The Messiah Himself predicted it & told Him... This is clear indication of Yahsah's merciful love for us... He did not condemn or judge Peter but rather made him the Rock on which the Church should stand & gave him the keys to the Kingdom of Heaven... Messiah knows how difficult it will be for us but our contrite hearts will convict us in our weakness & we will be strengthened by The Holy Spirit in these times... We will not be afraid but have courage to spread The Gospel to all...

Day 315: One with The Father & The Son...

John 14, 15, 16, 17

It is a true relief, blessing, assurance & promise for all those doing the work for The Father in the name of Yahsah The Messiah... We are to be perfected in one... There is Only One El Almighty...& there is Only One Son... They are One in as much as we are one with Them... only those who are doing the True Will of the Father... "This is everlasting life: Taking in knowledge of You YHWH, The One True El & The One Whom You sent forth, Yahsah The Messiah" JOHN 17:3...

Day 316: The Son of YHWH crucified for us...

Matthew 27; Mark 15

The heavens & earth quaked... the temple veil tore in two... the rocks were split... darkness filled the land... many saints arose from the dead appearing to many... What a scene to marvel... How astonishing, astounding & amazing to have beheld yet those on the side of Yahsah & The Father would also have felt anguished, wounded & grieved... However Our Messiah died to save our souls... that all those believing in His Name (Yahsah = Yah is Salvation) will not perish but gain everlasting life... He endured reviling, rebuke, offence, insult, abuse, mockery, derision & finally crucifixion... not for Himself but for us... He went through all that for us as the exemplary obedient Son of His Father... Look at the state of this world because of evil doers & those worshipping idols... & through all this The Messiah still shows mercy & died for every single one of us... "It is not YHWH's will that any should perish but that all should come to repentance" — 2 PETER 3:9...

Day 317: Our heart saves or condemns us...

Luke 23; John 18, 19

The Scriptures associated with this note are extremely profound needing intense meditation... First you have the condemnation of Israel as prophesied by The Messiah as He hung on the cross surrounded by the weeping women... He exclaimed "Do not weep for me but for yourselves & your children"... The very Jews who murdered Him are the very Jews of the Twelve Tribes of Israel... Their hearts were dark & evil though their behaviour may have appeared to some as righteous... It is those, their forefathers & their generations The Messiah was referring to... Their condemnation is grave & devastating... Then we have the salvation even of those who sin to the last moment... asking forgiveness not through lip service but from the true belief in their heart that Yahsah is The Messiah The Son of YHWH Almighty... The robber on the cross next to The Messiah knew He was The Saviour... He believed it without a doubt & even though He hung for the sin he had committed Yahsah knew his heart was good & he believed in Him... I love this scripture... It is the perfect epitome of mercy & forgiveness... The Messiah did not judge him but rewarded his heart, loyalty & unfailing belief... Beautiful...

Day 318: At the Right Hand of YHWH...

Matthew 28; Mark 16

Yahsah The Messiah was received up into Heaven on the 3rd day and sits on the Right Hand of The Father... To all trinitarians out there this scripture refutes this absurd, ludicrous & demonic doctrine... The Messiah sent His 12 Disciples out instructing them to make disciples of all the nation teaching them to observe all things that He commanded... The Messiah never once taught that He was The Father or The Holy Spirit... In fact He stated that The Father is greater than Him (JOHN 14:28)... It really comes down to not being in the Spirit of The Almighty to all those who continue to believe in this false trinitarian doctrine... There is no excuse... Search for the Truth & do not be misled by false teachers, preachers & prophets otherwise you will always be limited in your faith & never move any further in your Spiritual journey... Listen to your heart & be led by your Creator who is able to do all things... With men SOME things are possible... but with YHWH Almighty ALL things are possible... Amen!

Day 319: The Gospels…

Luke 24; John 20, 21

What a blessing to experience The Messiah through these Gospels… I have read through them 4 times now & every time YHWH reveals something new to me pertinent to my walk with The Messiah… Thank You so much Father for allowing Your Son to die & live again for us… Thank You so much my Saviour Yahsah for opening up the Scriptures to me & giving me life like I have never known…

Day 320: Receiving Holy Spirit...

Acts 1, 2, 3

The Holy Spirit is a gift only from The Father... Yahsah Himself revealed this to His Disciples saying He will pray to The Father & He shall send a Comforter The Spirit of Truth (JOHN 14:16, 17)... This Spirit gives Truth to all YHWH's Children... It is possible to receive Spiritual guidance from the Father but The Holy Spirit can only reside in a clean heart... There is a distinction between being guided by Spirit & being endued by Holy Spirit... Once we receive The Holy Spirit it is impossible to refute The Truth... This is what sets apart YHWH's Children... His Lost Sheep... These will do His Will & continue the Commands given to The Messiah preached to the people... The Holy Spirit is given only to those loyal to The Father & listening to His Son... No one hearing knowledge of The Truth yet continuing to follow false doctrines has The Holy Spirit in them... It would both be contradictory & impossible... YHWH's Children are set apart from this world... They are royal... They are peculiar... They are obedient... They are loyal to Him & His Truth...

Day 321: 'YAHSAH'... no other name...

Acts 4, 5, 6

YAHSAH means "Yah is salvation" derived from His Father's name YaHWaH meaning "He causes to become"... "For there is NO other name under heaven given to men by which we must be saved" — ACTS 4:12... The name given is YAHSAH... NOT Jesus... Jesus is a transliteration & possesses no meaning... This name change is one of Satan's biggest deception along with all the major churches in the world... If they teach the name of Jesus by which we are saved, the name of Jehovah as The Father, the trinity & any other false doctrine not found in the True Hebrew Scriptures then they are not of YHWH... & certainly do not have Holy Spirit... "He who has an ear let him hear what the Spirit says to the churches" — REVELATION 2:7... "Ask & it will be given... seek & you will find... knock & it will be opened to you" — MATTHEW 7:7...

Day 322: Thank You Father YHWH…

Acts 7, 8

YHWH Almighty… The Most High… Father of YAHSAH our Messiah… Our Father who art in Heaven… Thank You for making Yourself known to me… Thank You for Your gift of Your Holy Spirit… Thank You for revealing to me Your Love, Wisdom, Knowledge & Understanding… Thank You that I do not have to worry about a single thing because You take care of my every need… Thank You that You have given me 2 very beautiful daughters, 1 exceptionally beautiful granddaughter & by your mercy a handsome grandson-to-be… Thank You that You are in the very midst of my beautiful offspring, my siblings & my mother… Thank You for being so merciful & forgiving towards me… Thank You for loving me so much You gave Your Son as a sacrifice so I can live for eternity with Him & with You… Thank You for never forsaking me & being The best Father I could ever have… Thank You for entrusting me to do Your Work & being long-suffering in the process… Thank You for giving me the strength to continue despite the enemy attacks I have to endure… Thank You for truly being my Father… Amen!

Day 323: YHWH is the Cleanser...

Acts 9, 10

It is clear in the times before The Messiah many sacrificial laws were written pertaining to foods, rituals, etc... But these were overridden by the birth of The Messiah... The 10 Commandments still stand but the sacrificial laws were done away with because The Messiah Himself became the ultimate sacrifice... once & for all time... "What YHWH has cleansed we must not call unclean"... The eating of 'unclean' food is a sacrificial law but Paul declares in 1 TIMOTHY 4:3,4... "Food which YHWH created is to be received with thanksgiving by those who believe & know the Truth... For every creature of YHWH is good & NOTHING is to be refused if it is received with thanksgiving... for it is sanctified by The Word of YHWH & prayer"... The Father can make anything that is unclean clean through our prayers in Faith & Truth... Amen!

Day 324: Thank YHWH The Spirit is willing…

Acts 11, 12

You know Your Children YHWH by their hearts… I thank You Father that You lead all of Your Children for they know Your voice…

Day 325: Paul... Prophet to the Gentiles...

Acts 13, 14

Paul had certainly been given a great mission alongside his fellow disciples to preach the Good News of the Gospel of Yahsah to all the world... the Gentiles... They surely listened and many have given their lives to The Father... but the Jews were jealous of what was taking place so that Paul had to remind them of why YHWH sought favour in the Gentiles giving them the right to everlasting life as well... The Jews in their wickedness stoned Paul after he recounted their evil towards The Messiah by having Him crucified... Paul and Barnabas did a fine works for The Father that they were seen as gods named Hermes and Zeus respectively and given offerings of sacrifice... This offended Paul greatly that he tore his clothes and reproved the crowd telling them that they are as human as everyone else... that their offerings and worshipping of false gods was exactly what they were preaching against and giving understanding to turn away from... It is clear that they had not felt the Spirit of YHWH and had been conditioned in the teachings of mythical gods... but Paul did not give up educating the Gentiles... for indeed this was the calling given to him by YHWH The Father...

Day 326: James speaks volumes...

James 1, 2, 3, 4, 5

JAMES is one of very few books in the bible where I could literally highlight every verse in every chapter... It is so in depth & full of instructions that are so very pertinent to today as much as it was when he wrote them... James, the brother of The Messiah, was indeed filled with The Holy Spirit & truly understood the nature of the fleshly man... My psychological understanding of the mind & how we as humans develop habits is described here in his book... It's amazing because I am assured I share the same spirit as James... All of YHWH's Children will come together in One Spirit... How beautiful... JAMES is a must read needing profound meditation...

Day 327: YHWH never forsakes us… we forsake Him…

Acts 15, 16

We serve such an Almighty Precious El who promises to take care of our every need… When we make decisions to put off following His Ways we deny ourselves of His grace, blessings & love… Then we don't understand why things are not going well & start to blame The Father saying, "where are You?"… He says "I will never leave you nor forsake you so you may boldly say… 'The FATHER is my helper, whom shall I fear, what can man do to me?'" — HEBREWS 13:5,6… Follow The Messiah with all your heart & do not doubt… Accept the Gift of Life that YHWH has promised… He never goes back on His promises…

Day 328: The Messiah lives in me...

Galatians 1, 2, 3

These Scriptures truly depicts the life we experience when we fully accept our calling... We are no longer tied to the world... We no longer think like the world does... We no longer understand relationships on a fleshly level... We will know when we are Messiah-like when all we long to do is follow the Ways of Yahsah The Messiah & minister for YHWH... When we are truly living by faith we have truly come to know that our Father & Messiah are real... Then we experience the realisation of the love They have for us... That The Messiah actually gave His life for us... How beautiful my Saviour is & how blessed I am to be one with Him & The Father...

Day 329: Reap what you sow...

Galatians 4, 5, 6

Paul marched as a loyal soldier of The Messiah... diligently fulfilling the ministerial work commissioned by YHWH our Father... In his letters to the Galatians he was expanding their understanding of the law and faith... The law pertains to the things of the flesh & therefore YHWH's righteous are not justified by it... Instead they are justified by the faith they have in The Messiah... Think about it... Many 'Christians' keep the law but through lack of faith their hearts are cold... Therefore will they inherit the Kingdom of YHWH? It is faith working through love that avails... Love is the fulfilment of the law... When we live in the Spirit we walk according to the Spirit... love, peace, joy, log-suffering, kindness, gentleness, faithfulness & self-control... against which the fleshly things have no hold over us... It is the desire for fleshly things that leads us into temptation because Satan can only use the flesh to tempt us & lead us away from YHWH... away from our salvation & the very thing our Messiah died for... What we reap is what we sow… Sow in good soil (The Spirit) & you reap everlasting life & peace… But sow in corruptible soil (the flesh) & you reap torment, death & a place in Satan's kingdom… The flesh is an enmity to YHWH & has no place with Him… YHWH is Spirit… not flesh… The flesh means nothing to Him… We live in our flesh bodies here on earth so have to have provisions for the body which YHWH supplies without any effort on our part… He wants us then to focus purely on our Spirit so the flesh has no power… "Seek first YHWH's Kingdom & His Righteousness & ALL other things will be added to us" — MATTHEW 6:33… If we truly love our Father & truly love His Son Yahsah The Messiah our desire will be to do Their will & therefore concentrate primarily, predominantly & passionately on the things of The Spirit… Just as this is my desire & my prayer daily for myself I pray that this is also the desire of all those professing faith in The Messiah…

Day 330: YHWH not in dwellings made of hands...

Acts 17

What a something... the Greeks serving false gods actually had an altar inscribed, "To The Unknown Mighty One"... with no idea of Whom this referred to... However Paul was given an opportunity to speak before these Greeks who liked hearing fresh teachings... Paul gave them understanding of 'The Unknown Mighty One' and His Son concluding the everlasting gift of salvation... Many mocked him but many also believed and put faith as due to his proclamation... Paul made it known that YHWH is The Almighty Spiritual El who does not reside in dwellings made by human hands or has any need of man to satisfy Him... He Himself gives to ALL life... ALL breath... ALL else... Paul emphatically encouraged them to reach out and find Yahsah and The Father for They are not far from us...

Day 331: **Do not grow weary...**

1 Thessalonians **1, 2, 3, 4, 5**

It is a privilege & a pleasure to have a desire & to be called & chosen to do the work for YHWH... My ministry started Friday 26 September 2014... I have made a vow to open my home every Friday & dedicate myself to ministering the Word in Fellowship to YHWH's Faithful Females though all are truly welcomed... This is His commission & one I accept with great responsibility... I make myself available whilst He makes me able... I am also so fortunate & blessed that I have a family who believe & are willing to come together in regular fellowship... However to minister YHWH's Word I need to be fully immersed in His Holy Spirit... I have to fast in order to gain the Power of His Spirit in Wisdom, Knowledge, Understanding & Love... This is a weekly dedication that takes a lot of energy & focus which leaves me exhausted at times... There are moments when labouring to do YHWH's work is received with complacency & it's these times I understand why Paul encourages us not to grow weary in doing good... We as ministers are merely sowers of seeds... It is YHWH who waters & grows... In order to continue in strength doing the work for YHWH I remind myself of my own journey with my Saviour to The Father & the time it has taken to get to where I am today... I gave my life willingly & with a deep desire to The Father in 2001... Patience, perseverance & love are the key... Love for YHWH our Father The Most High... love for His Son our Blessed Saviour Yahsah The Messiah... & love for all those with a willingness to receive The Word of YHWH...

Day 332: I AM with you...

Acts 18, 19

YHWH always comes through... He is The Almighty after all... When He makes Himself known to you there really is no turning back... It is apparent that He & His Son are real & knowing this can never be undone... They direct your whole life... everything you say... everything you feel... every you do... Leave everything to Them & you can never fail... There is a part of me that feels burdened with the things of this world... & that part is my flesh... But what liberation & revitalisation to be able to speak freely about my Father & my Saviour... Fear no longer plays a part... zeal takes over & becomes the energy fuelled by Holy Spirit... I will not be afraid... I will speak... I will not keep silent... I will share The Truth to those YHWH sends me... & The Truth is YHWH The Most High El & Yahsah The Messiah Saviour of The World...

Day 333: The Mind of The Messiah…

1 Corinthians 1, 2, 3, 4

1 Corinthians is an immensely revealing book so far but the 2nd Chapter is so far the most powerful… YHWH is not concerned with wisdom belonging to the flesh… carnal or worldly… For the wisdom of this world is foolishness with YHWH (1 Corinthians 3:19)… He concerns Himself only with the Wisdom of Spiritual things… & this Wisdom we can only receive through His Holy Spirit… Those who have the Mind of The Messiah do not contend with each other but reason all things in peace & with unity in The Spirit… Those not having the Mind of The Messiah will never understand the things of YHWH's Spirit because it is the Spirit that discerns all things… Therefore contention & strife will always exist with this population… The true desire to have the Mind of The Messiah opens up our hearts to receive the free gift of the Holy Spirit & therefore revealing to us the deep things of YHWH that no fleshly man can attain… "No one knows the things of YHWH except the Spirit of YHWH" — 2:11… "The Kingdom of YHWH is not in word but in power" — 4:20… This true Power & the mysteries of YHWH will always be shared with love & gentleness… Amen to YHWH our Father… Amen to Yahsah The Messiah… & Amen to all the saints doing the work for the glory of YHWH & The Lamb…

Day 334: Unrighteous inherit no Kingdom...

1 Corinthians 5, 6, 7, 8

In this world speaking about homosexuality from a spiritual perspective is a very touchy, sensitive matter... There are many 'Christians' who condemn homosexuals because of their own misunderstanding of Scriptures pertaining to this group... However there are many who fall into the group of unrighteousness yet why do they not receive the same persecutory damnation? This attack on homosexuals has given rise to the term 'homophobia' as a result & anyone not accepting homosexuality apparently are deemed homophobic... What I have now come to realise is unrighteousness is a result of adversarial spiritual persuasion... If YHWH being The Creator opposes the act of homosexuality (because it is the behaviour & NOT the person YHWH abhors)... it is impossible that YHWH would create a person as such... therefore what makes a person 'gay'? We are intrinsically spiritual beings therefore governed by spirit... When we behave in ways that go against YHWH's Laws then it is the spirit of destruction leading us… but this is unbeknown to all those not of YHWH's Spirit & to a lot of those who 'believe' they are of His Spirit… When we are doing the things that are right in YHWH's Eyes we are being guided by His Holy Spirit… Satan's biggest deception is not just making the world believe that YHWH The Creator doesn't exist but that he himself doesn't exist… Satan is the father of deception & can make any lie appear as truth… Many homosexuals believe they are born as such… thus it is their truth… This is the intention of Satan… because he wants to destroy as many people as he can… Remember it is not YHWH's will that any should perish but that all should come to repentance… As Children of YHWH all we can do is give this message in the hope that many will hear, understand & be saved… Give this message with love & gentleness asking always for the Power of Holy Spirit for guidance… The things of The Spirit far exceeds the wisdom of man… This is no easy task… Thus the Power of The Spirit is an absolute necessity…

Day 335: What is idolatry??...

1 Corinthians 9, 10, 11

Idolatry is the partaking of anything that is a displeasure to YHWH... It is the worship, focus or devotion to fleshly things, false doctrines, Pagan festivals, religions other than The Way of The Messiah, etc... YHWH set aside traditions for His people to follow... Passover, Communion, Sabbath... but only if all are observing His Ways fully... So then what has Christmas, Easter & Valentine got to do with The Messiah & The Father? Absolutely nothing... These are fleshly celebrations... & it's not difficult to evidence this as practically the whole of the Western world celebrates it most of which don't even exercise faith in our Father YHWH or His Son... Messiah was not born on the 25th December... no-one knows exactly when He was born... The Christmas tree is a symbol of idolatry... The giving of presents as part of this festival is an indulgent gratification of the flesh... This festival replicates the account of The Two Witnesses in REVELATION 11... YHWH is not concerned with any freshly thing... He requires a good conscience towards Him which comes from True Love... & not the giving in to the things of the flesh or secular celebrations... The fact that the major churches of today endorse it is evidence of their teaching in error... The spirit of Christmas belongs to the master of the flesh... This master is the father of perdition... Satan... do not be taken in by him... "Therefore my beloved, flee from idolatry" — 1 CORINTHIANS 10:14

Day 336: The Greatest Gift... LOVE...

1 Corinthians 12, 13, 14

I LOVE this chapter... It is a perfect depiction of the meaning of love... This is not the love that the world knows... for the love of the world lacks spiritual depth... The closest to this love in a worldly sense is the love of a parent for their child... an unconditional love that no matter what the child does wrong or the mistakes they make they are disciplined, chastised & reproved but the love still remains... To discipline, chastise & reprove is to give understanding of the wrong, to allow opportunity for learning & the time to make the right changes... Only the Holy Spirit knows these things so it is This Spirit that gives all the guidance... It is easy to show this unconditional love to our children & those who we are very close to... but how easy is it to show this love to colleagues, acquaintances, strangers, church members, neighbours etc especially when their words & deeds goes against the Ways of YHWH & pushes the wrong buttons in us... Only our desire to please YHWH & the wisdom of The Holy Spirit can help us do what is right in the Eyes of our Creator... that is to do all things with love... The Greatest Gift of All...

Day 337: Working for YHWH...

1 Corinthians 15, 16

I look back on my journey in faith and remember challenging my brother in various aspect of the Walk with YHWH... At times it would get very heated... We would even fall out because I wouldn't agree with the content or his approach... Years later I can now understand & agree with a lot of what he was sharing... His approach is much more effective now also... although I think his wife may disagree... He is a devout man of YHWH striving to always do the Work for YHWH... He has always tried to encourage others to do the same... including me... I used to believe it was not for everyone & gave personal testimonies & witnessing as my contribution... I focused on my career first then on doing the Work for YHWH second... Now that has all changed 180 degrees... What I can do & what I want to do for YHWH supersedes any secular work... I know that putting my YHWH first He will without doubt take care of all my needs... I still have a focus on an enterprise that utilises the gifts, wisdom & knowledge YHWH has supplied me with... but all to the greater good of my Father... I love that I have arrived here in this spiritual realm & that nearly all my brother spoke of then that I found challenging & alarming makes sense to me now... It has taught me that unless YHWH has revealed His Mysteries through His Holy Spirit some things are not going to make sense at the time... to me or others... but we must put all things in prayer asking YHWH to give us The Truth according to His Ways... the Way that The Messiah demonstrated & taught so we may have conferred on us our reward... an Everlasting Life of Peace & Love with our Father & His Son...

Day 338: Unseen things = Eternity...

2 Corinthians 1, 2, 3, 4

It really is the time of reckoning... It is time to get right with The Father... Continuing to do the things according to the flesh means we remain in the flesh & the knowledge & wisdom available to us is that which is seen & understood by the world... It is not deep but superficial... on the surface & undoubtedly temporal... But when we immerse ourselves in the Spirit of YHWH... the daily reading of His Words, constant meditation & prayer, obedience to His Commands, Statutes, Regulations & the Teachings of His Holy Spirit... then we are privilege to the Deep Things of YHWH... the unseen wisdom, revealed to those following The Ways of The Messiah with trueness of heart... This cannot be seen by the world because these are revealed in the depths of the heart that has already found its place in eternal existence... without doubt & with no lacking of faith... It is this that enables us to see the unseen things leading to a life of eternal peace & love...

Day 339: Be pleasing to YHWH...

2 Corinthians 5, 6, 7, 8, 9

There is no escape for anyone... all must give an accounting before YHWH for the things we have done in this life, both in righteousness & wickedness... So our aim in this life is to be well pleasing to YHWH... in the flesh & in the Spirit... Since we are in this world our Spirit is housed in our flesh... but we have to learn not to give into the desires of the flesh... self-gratification... When we have the desire to serve YHWH we no longer should have the desire to satisfy our flesh... That doesn't mean our flesh will stop yearning to be gratified... because it won't... the flesh & spirit will always be at war with each other... It means that we learn to understand that the yearning flesh is by manipulation of the gods of this world... the dark spirits wanting to keep our focus on the world in an attempt to distract us & take our focus away from YHWH therefore our focus on salvation... When we focus on the flesh we continue to make it stronger & the spirit becomes weaker... we are then more susceptible to be used by the wicked one... When we focus on the Father & His Spiritual gifts we strengthen our Spirit & so the flesh becomes weaker therefore less desirous & in need of satisfying... We then hear The Spirit of YHWH clearly leading us to His Perfect Peace, Love & Wisdom... We are habitual beings as created by YHWH... therefore "practice makes progress"... Keep on doing the things pleasing to YHWH & live for The Messiah who died & was risen up for us (2 CORINTHIANS 5:15)...

Day 340: Glory in YHWH...

2 Corinthians 10, 11, 12, 13

My glory is in my Father YHWH... You my Father & Your Son are the only Ones I can truly trust who will never let me down... If the truth be known the walk with You is a difficult one... but walking in the flesh before giving my life to You was even harder... Why? Because I was contending in my own strength & losing... it was tiring... Now You contend for me because You love me & want what's best for me now & for eternity... The adversary is powerful... there is no denying this... & only You can defeat Him... You already have by giving us Your Son... Those who have made an earnest vow to walk with The Messiah will need to rely on You... through obedience to Your Word with Love... The enemy will always want to contend with us because he knows he has lost & his aim is to destroy as many of Your Children as he can... But You Oh Father promise not let this happen... You will never leave us nor forsake us... My faith is always & forever in You my Father & my Messiah... All glory & love to You...

Day 341: Living by Faith...

Romans 1, 2, 3

The Messiah said to 'doubting' Thomas "Because you have seen Me you believe... but blessed are those who have not seen yet believe" — JOHN 20:29... This is a true epitome of living in faith... Our hearts convict us that The Messiah & The Father are real... It is the Holy Spirit that convicts our hearts... But without faith our minds would be closed & we would therefore cut off communication with The Spirit... "Faith is the assured expectation of things to come and the evident reality though not yet beheld" — HEBREWS 11:1... When we lose faith or have no faith we lose all & do not have the opportunity of receiving all YHWH's love & wisdom which only the Holy Spirit gives... YHWH's gifts are only for those who believe & exercise faith in The Messiah... True faith is knowing for sure that The Messiah & The Father are real & that Their love for us therefore is also real...

Day 342: Mind vs. flesh...

Romans 4, 5, 6, 7

The mind is in constant battle with the flesh... this is what leads to temptation & then to sin if first one is unable to discern & second if one is weak therefore unable to resist the temptation... It is the love YHWH & His Son has for us and the love we have for Them in return that strengthens us, gives us wisdom & discernment therefore enabling us to resist temptation... The love we have for The Father & The Son convicts our hearts & compels us to do the right thing... but our hearts have to be filled by Holy Spirit for this process to occur continually & so it can only be filled when we are walking according to the Spirit... that means reading & being a doer of The Word with desire & faith... It is a dynamic process that continues throughout our walk in this present life... Our flesh is transient & attached to the things of this world... our spirit is eternal... Whether we earn the gift of eternal life or the wages of sin leading to death depends on the control of our minds... Live for YHWH & the Holy Spirit is your guide... but live for the flesh & the things of this world & unfortunately Satan is your guide just by default alone... His dark spirits & angels manipulate the mind & without the wisdom & love from the Holy Spirit you will not be able to discern... you will be under compulsion operating through non-conscious awareness... Live in YHWH's Spirit & let The Holy Spirit guide your mind...

Day 343: Live in The Spirit...

Romans 8, 9, 10

It is impossible to live according to the flesh & call ourselves "Sons of YHWH"... There is no escaping from the Truth of The Word but many people attempt to... They would rather please men (friends, family, congregation, pastors, colleagues etc.) than The Creator YHWH Almighty... The proof is in the choices we make, the depth of search for The Truth & our conviction... It takes courage to make a stand for YHWH's Truth because it puts you in a minority fighting against ALL the world religions... there are few in this category... The Word evidences it... "Wide is the gate & broad is the way that leads to destruction & many go through it... but narrow is the gate & difficult is the way leading to life & only a few shall find it" — MATTHEW 7:14... Christmas, Valentine, Easter etc. are all things of the flesh... It's clearly evidenced by the following of almost all the Western world & a significant amount globally & by the consumerism attached to it... I know that many who say they are 'godly' follow these traditions which are founded in Paganism... Pleading ignorance after hearing the facts cannot save you... "The fleshly mind is an enmity against YHWH... so those in the flesh cannot please Him" — ROMANS 8:7,8... Choose life in The Spirit... or choose death in the flesh... That's it in a nutshell...!!!

Day 344: Live peaceably...

Romans 11, 12, 13

The book of Romans contains two of my favourite chapters, chapter 12 being one of them... I could easily have highlighted the whole chapter & on reflection I almost have... I have known about these verses for many years... Verse 9 through to 21 resonates strongly with me... The message of love & peace towards all is emphasised vehemently here... We can often get caught out in the midst of heightened emotional arousal because more often than not irrational thoughts are produced... I.e. when feeling upset, angered, frustrated, irritated etc. The dark spirits uses these emotionally fuelled situations to machinate by contaminating the mind with irrational, harmful thoughts that lead to feelings of resentment, emptiness, rejection, betrayal etc. These responses are habitual & most likely stem from childhood experiences... Left with these feelings the easiest thing to do is think ill of the person who you believe is responsible even though we are responsible for the way we think, feel or act... otherwise when the time comes to give an account to YHWH we would be putting blame on a lot of other people... When we experience these heightened emotions it's usually because we feel hurt or fear... If we take time out to address & learn to understand our pain & fear we can then learn to respond rationally... & in the way YHWH intends... "Being kindly affection to one another with brotherly love… as much as depends on us living peaceably with all men" — ROMANS 12:10, 18… We need to stop conforming to this world & be transformed by the renewing of our minds… Oh My El YHWH, I know for certain none of this is possible unless we are truly in Your Spirit Father… When we are in Your Spirit our vulnerabilities & weaknesses will not govern our relationships… We will realise that everyone has vulnerabilities & indispositions & to recognise our own & embrace them is what strengthens us & makes us beautiful… Then for the Love of The Creator & His Son we will seek peace to glorify Them in order to continue saving souls… Our reward comes from Them & that's what matters… When we please our Kings we by default please man… at least those who share the same spirit — ROMANS 12:16!!!

Day 345: Acceptable to YHWH...

Romans 14, 15, 16

I love my Father YHWH & I love my Saviour Yahsah The Messiah... With Them is everything you need in life... beautiful & amazing... safe & secure... But there are adversities to encounter also... "Heirs of YHWH & joint heirs with The Messiah if indeed we suffer with Him that we may also be glorified together" — ROMANS 8:17... I am aware that many of those who say they believe & worship YHWH & The Messiah do so in a 'convenient' way to themselves... They are 'selective' with the scriptures they follow & would rather accept the doctrines of man on behalf of the church than the doctrines of YHWH... Some believe what they are told in their hearts because they know no better yet... & others because they want to fit in... They want to belong regardless of hearing the truth... Everyone will have to give an accounting & many will not be in that number sitting on the right hand of The Messiah... Loyalty to The Father & The Son should never be a convenience but a worship in Spirit & in Truth (JOHN 4:24)... It is peace & joy in The Holy Spirit serving The Messiah... In this we are acceptable to YHWH... but only those who truly have the Holy Spirit will walk with loyalty in the Commands & Laws of YHWH... YHWH has not changed... the world has in their worship of Him... It is evidently clear who are His Children & who are not once the truth has been spoken & heard...

Day 346: Wake up to the Truth of YHWH...

Acts 20, 21, 22, 23

Oh the irony... The Holy Spirit is The Spirit of Truth... It can only give the truth & nothing else... All the Truth of YHWH is revealed by His Holy Spirit that dwells only in the hearts of those who have been cleansed... There are ministering spirits that speak to our spirit but The Holy Spirit dwells only within a Holy Temple... so anyone who has been cleansed by The Word, has a good conscience towards YHWH, exercises faith in Messiah, walks according to His Commands in the Spirit & does not wilfully or knowingly practising sin... To be a teacher, apostle, disciple, preacher & evangelist for YHWH takes years of training, dedication, devotion & cleansing by YHWH... A medical doctor studies for years to be fully trained... & then to specialise he studies even more... Then to be a consultant more years... & then even more years to become a professor... Once he is trained it would take a foolish trainee or junior doctor to contend with the knowledge of the doctor that is a specialist, consultant or professor... It is the same as one who is advanced in The Spirit... A new Follower of The Messiah or one who has not been taught the Word by the Spirit, still drinking milk, would be foolish to contend with one who is mature, eating meat &

sanctified by YHWH through The Holy Spirit… Paul laboured through constant adversities preaching The Truth of YHWH… He warned of false doctrines, perversions & savage wolves entering into the churches… & it's clear this has taken place… "Therefore remember that I did not cease to warn everyone night & day with tears… therefore I testify that I am innocent of the blood of all men" — ACTS 20:31,26… "Who can make an accusation against YHWH's elect? He sanctifies them… He declares them righteous" — ROMANS 8:33… Let your hearts be convicted by The Holy Spirit & not by man… praying always to the Creator our Father YHWH Almighty for the Truth… The irony is that this Truth will be seen by many as false & perverse… But the truth is the major churches of the world, deriving fundamentally from the Roman Church, has been fooling everyone for centuries… it's now time to wake up to their perversion… I speak only to those who are in the church… To those out of the church they have possibly escaped the conditioning & corruption of these organised businesses by YHWH's grace… Research & do not leave your salvation in anyone else's hands… but in YHWH's & His Precious Son…

Day 347: Giving thanks...

Acts 24, 25, 26

Thank You Father for this Sabbath rest... Thank You Father for calling me & choosing me 2 do Your Will... Thank You for preparing a place for me in Your Kingdom... Thank you Father for Your Holy Spirit that teaches me all Your Truths... Thank You Father for my very beautiful girls that You have given me as a gift & precious fruits to steward... Thank You Father that I still have the family I grew up in & that they know of You... Thank You for The Saviour of the world that is Your Beloved Son Yahsah & my Messiah... Thank You Yahsah The Messiah my Beloved for laying down Your life for me... Thank You Both for Your loving-kindness, Your Wisdom, Your Peace, Your knowledge, Your protection & Your Joy... Thank You for bringing me from the dead & giving me life...

Day 348: Salvation open to all...

Acts 27, 28

I don't have to imagine what Paul went through in terms of convincing Israel the Truth about The Messiah because I encounter this experience regularly... The Truth Paul had was given to Him by The Holy Spirit... unadulterated & wise... If you have an ear to hear, eyes to see & a heart to understand you will be convicted by the truth of the Holy Spirit... Paul spoke to Israel... these are those that professed worship to YHWH, knew about The Messiah yet rejected Him... Paul was then sent to the rest of the world, the Gentiles, so that they could have a part in the Promise... Today the hearts of those in the churches have grown dull... They have brought into the lie & worshipping in error... I was too... but The Holy Spirit convicted me of the Truth... thank YHWH... My loyalty was to Him & His Son... I sought Their approval & not the leaders of the church... It really is simple... those in The Holy Spirit of YHWH hearing, seeing & understanding His Truth & that of His True Son Yahsah The Messiah have their names written in the Book of Life & a place in The Kingdom... the rest do not!!!!

Day 349: Put on Love...

Colossians 1, 2, 3, 4; Philemon 1

I am having such an amazing journey walking with The Messiah & The Father... "Blessed is the man whose delight is in the law of YHWH & in His law he meditates night & day" — PSALMS 1:1... Everyday YHWH reveals His wisdom... He unfolds more of His Mysteries & understandings about Himself, His Son & His creation to me... To know love you truly have to know The Father... The love of The Father means pleasing Him & accepting His Requirements... He has a Chosen Race but their relentless disobedience meant YHWH's Eternal Promise was given to all humanity... However those not of The True Vine have to be taught about their Creator... not with judgement or condemnation but with mercy, long-suffering & love... In order to teach them you need to have accurate knowledge of The Truth but this will never be gained from today's churches because we know for fact they are teaching in error if they uphold the doctrines of trinity, the name Jesus & Jehovah & festivals such as Christmas, Easter & Valentines... If you truly love YHWH & His Son these experiences of idolatry would be far from you... I'm not saying that your love for Them is fake... I'm saying your love has not been perfected... I have truly come to understand why it is imperative to delight in the Law of YHWH & meditate on it day & night because without it you will never come to know The Father or The Son therefore your salvation is in jeopardy... The Holy Spirit makes known the Truth of YHWH to all HIs Children through The Word because YHWH knows those who truly love Him & are willing to accept His Way above everything else in the world... "If you were raised with The Messiah then seek those things above where The Messiah is sitting at the right hand of YHWH... set your mind on things above & not things on earth" — COLOSSIANS 3:1,2... Put on Perfect Love...

Day 350: The Whole Armour of YHWH...

Ephesians 1, 2, 3, 4, 5

As Followers of The Messiah it is so important to understand that all our trials & tribulations are necessary to increase our endurance & faith (JAMES 1)... When we experience contention in our relationships remember it may appear personal but be very clear that our conflict is not against flesh & blood... it is against principalities & powers, against the rulers of darkness in this age, against the wicked spiritual hosts in the heavenly places... Satan's mission is to steal, kill & destroy... The only way he can do this is through our minds... We have to learn to understand the function of the mind in order to discern when Satan's spirits are machinating through the manipulation of our thoughts in order to deceive us... When we harbour bitterness, grudges & unkind thoughts towards each other Satan uses this to create further animosity & contention within us & between us... All of us are susceptible to being used by Satan... but if we can understand the function of the mind we can discern our thoughts & change any unhelpful thinking into helpful healthy ones & help those who we contend with or who contend with us to understand this too... Our thoughts lead to feelings... our feelings lead to urges... & our urges lead to behaviours... If our thoughts are unhelpful then we will feel bad... & if we are feeling bad then we have an urge to act it out... then our behaviour as a consequence will reflect this... We may do things that are detrimental & sinful then end up regretting it... YHWH's Words helps us to understand this through the refining process... The Word cleanses us & as a result the Holy Spirit which is the Spirit of Truth dwells within us... This Spirit gives us wisdom & discernment helping us to do what is right... this is fundamental to our faith... "Put on the whole armour of YHWH that you maybe able to stand against the wiles of Satan" — EPHESIANS 6:11... (WILES = a trick intended to deceive or ensnare)...

Day 351: YHWH is faithful to complete a good work in you...

Philippians 1, 2, 3, 4

These four chapters are truly wonderful scriptures... so much to offer... so much to take in... YHWH truly will complete a good work in all those who are sincere to His Words given to us by His Son Yahsah The Messiah... That indeed was the case for Paul who went out to the Gentiles to do his good work of delivering The Good News of The Gospel... Paul experienced the highs and the lows... He spoke of having an abundance and of having nothing... to both having excess and having need but enduring through it all with humility and actually being content regardless of how tough it became... why? Because he had a true love for the Messiah and The Father Who sent Him... Paul gives wonderful messages of how we should be as a true follower of The Messiah and encouragement of how to sustain our mental health... Do not be anxious for anything but in all things pray to The Father whatever it is we need... being thankful regardless... and the promise? That The Father will give us a peace that goes beyond any human understanding so that our mental and emotional health is protected... that we truly feel safe and secure because we truly know The Father and The Son... And so Paul tells us to meditate constantly on all those things that are good... whatever is noble... righteous... lovely... clean... pure... of good report... these are a pleasure and praiseworthy to YHWH... remembering that He Who has begun a good work in us will be faithful to complete it...

Day 352: Carnal riches vs Spiritual riches...

1 Timothy 1, 2, 3, 4, 5

YHWH our Father is not carnal... He is Spirit... Therefore He has no affinity with or connection at all to the carnal, the secular or the fleshly things... "They are not of the world" — JOHN 17:14... "Do not be conformed by this world but be transformed by the renewing of your mind... that you may prove what is that good, acceptable and perfect Will of YHWH" — ROMANS 12:2... It grieves me when I see those who profess to be YHWH's Children running down the riches of the world believing that YHWH's blessings comes in fancy cars, designer clothes, mansions, precious jewellery, stocks & shares etc... These things are nothing to YHWH (1 TIMOTHY 6:6-10)... YHWH requires humility, mercy, righteousness, modesty & faith... A true faith in The Father means you will never worry about your needs being met because He promises to meet them all (MATTHEW 6:33... PHILLIPIANS 4:19)... Chasing the material things of this world is purely to gratify the flesh... These are the illusionary things of Satan trapping the mind leading those falling into the trap to perdition... Wake up... Wake up... Search... Stop leaving your salvation in the hands of man (PHILIPPIANS 2:12)... Seek the Spiritual riches that are eternal (MATTHEW 6:19-21)... Don't you know YHWH created precious stones & metals... In paradise they will be so abundant that our natural habitats will be unimaginably palatial... Man has taken His creation led by Satan &

attached high monetary value to it so that those that have can lord it over those that don't… & those that don't then lose their souls trying to gain it… This is Satan's aim… "Blessed are the poor for theirs is the Kingdom of Heaven… blessed are the meek for they shall inherit the earth" — MATTHEW 5:3,5… This life is transient… so short lived… Aim for eternity where true paradise & perfection is… perfect peace, perfect love, perfect joy… Life forever with our perfect beings… our beautiful Father & His beautiful Son… basking in true heavenly riches and glory…

Day 353: Matriarchal ministry...

Titus 1, 2, 3,

It is such an honour to serve YHWH... I would never have envisaged me in the position that I am in now... Since completing my Masters in counselling, after giving my life to YHWH & experiencing the distress of women sharing their struggles with me, it has been my desire to set up a fellowship ministering to women... Who would have known that it would be such a difficult path... but an incredibly powerful & rewarding one... "All things come together for good... to those who love YHWH... to those who are called according to His purpose" — ROMANS 8:28... I remember the resistance I encountered from many people in the church when I was studying towards my Bachelor degree in psychology... but I couldn't see what their problem was... Now I know it was the works of Satan (& some ignorance) attempting to veer me away from the path laid out by my Creator... I have learnt about the structure & the function of the mind & how this influences behaviour... I was given a wonderful opportunity to study psychotherapy which taught me the fundamental skills of helping individuals in times of trouble... However it is ultimately my walk with YHWH that has given me the Power to unlock the answers within each human being I come into contact with to enable them to truly "find themselves" in order to reach their full potential... the purpose of their existence... YHWH knows who they are & He will lead them to me... He knows I am available & able because He has made me capable...

Day 354: YHWH's Special People…

1 Peter 1, 2, 3, 4, 5

To be one of YHWH's Special People is an eternal honour… but who are His Special People? They are those who seek to please Him first before anyone or anything… who are truly obedient to His Word… who seek the Truth like searching for buried treasure & once finding it work diligently to minister to the rest of YHWH's People & all those with a willingness to hear so they too may find the Truth… These have come to understand that they were taken out of darkness from death into The Light which is in the Life & Love of our Father YHWH… The Love that is His Son our Living Saviour YAHSAH The Messiah…

Day 355: YHWH holds no record of wrongs…

Hebrews 1, 2, 3, 4, 5

I cannot believe that the NKJV & the KJV of the bible have removed the text, "[love] holds no record of wrongs" — 1 CORINTHIANS 13:5… I was glad to see however a similar text in Hebrews 10:17… "Their sins & their lawless deeds I will remember no more"… We serve such an almighty & merciful Father… He loves us so much & it's these traits He wants us to develop & manifest to others… Why? Because it stops the wiles of Satan having any effect in our lives… All of YHWH's Laws & Commandments were given to protect us… but the fleshly man sees them as a burden… a killer of pleasure… They don't know more than YHWH yet they have allowed Satan to fool them into believing they are above Him… more powerful… & that is their downfall into Sheol unless they turn away from their sins, ask for forgiveness & walk with true faith in YHWH's Righteous Way… I am so saddened when I see those who say they are in the Father fooled by Satan… I see so clearly that these have not been in the Word & have been living very much in the flesh… Satan relentlessly manipulates the mind of those holding on to the past & struggling to forgive others & themselves… They become tormented & attack those of the true brotherhood trying to help them… They make pain, torment & misery for themselves rather than humble at the mercy of YHWH doing what is right in His Eyes… wondering why they are still struggling with difficulty & desperation in their faith… Not worshipping in Spirit & Truth costs dearly… Children of YHWH who are not paying heed to His Commands will experience suffering until they start doing what is right in YHWH's Eyes…

Day 356: Chastisement leads to righteousness...

Hebrews 7, 8, 9, 10

I so enjoyed reading HEBREWS 12 today... I have a friend who is severely afflicted by Satan at present... I see the things that she is doing which are a displeasure to YHWH... When I shared the Word of YHWH with her highlighting His Commands in reference to what she is experiencing she attacked me saying I am dictating & being judgemental... What she failed to understand is that The Word judges (JOHN 12:48) & that she is being chastened by YHWH... But what a beautiful thing... because without chastening it means we are illegitimate, not loved & not Sons of YHWH (HEBREWS 12:8)...

Day 357: Faith... assured expectation... proof of reality not yet seen...

Hebrews 11, 12, 13

Such powerful chapters... not just of faith... but of favourable discipline and promises... to those who are the True, legitimate children of The Most High... They recounts the faith of all the great leaders before the 'earthly' birth of our Messiah... Noah, Abraham, Moses, David, Daniel, even Sarah and Rahab... These were all faithful to the end and have received their place in eternity with The Father & The Son... There is so much to gain from these readings... to encourage our continual faith because of the love we have for our Kings... Let us enjoy being in Their Fold... now and in the time to come...

Day 358: YHWH's servants to be gentle & patient...

2 Timothy 1, 2, 3, 4

I love 2 TIMOTHY chapter 2... It has so much wisdom for the servant doing YHWH's work... I am feeling so sad at present thinking of how Satan has committed a great deception through the high leaders of the churches today... I am absolutely astonished at the revelation of The Truth from my Father & knowing what I know now I am glad to come across this scripture guiding & encouraging me to give The Truth with gentleness, patience & humility... This is how Yahsah The Messiah gave it & as a Follower of The Messiah I too follow in His Steps, His Commands & His Ways... We cannot go wrong if we follow Him explicitly... Any traditions, festivals, celebrations not followed by The Messiah or YHWH's loyal people should not be adhered to by His Children today... "Nevertheless the solid foundation of YHWH stands having this seal... 'YHWH knows who are His... let everyone who names The Name of The Messiah depart from sin'" — 2 TIMOTHY 2:19 "All unrighteousness is sin" — 1 JOHN 5:17... Following pagan traditions is unrighteous therefore sinful...

Day 359: Moved by Holy Spirit....

2 Peter 1, 2, 3; Jude 1

6 more days left & I will have completed reading The Holy Scriptures in a year by the grace of YHWH... But it is evident the scriptures have been tampered with... words rewritten... sentences removed... texts added... Only The Holy Spirit can guide our reading of The Scriptures (2 PETER 1:20,21)... which is absolutely necessary for salvation (JAMES 1:21)... No one can have The Holy Spirit unless they are cleansed... The Word cleanses those who are true in their faith, adhering to the Word & worshipping YHWH The Creator in Spirit & Truth... Everything that is true of YHWH can be found in Scriptures... but interpretation is not private... It did not come from the will of man but Holy men spoke moved by Holy Spirit... You will know them by their fruits (MATTHEW 7:16)...

Day 360: The Love of YHWH...

1 John 1, 2, 3, 4, 5

Wow... There are many incredibly pertinent passages in the 1st Book of JOHN... especially for the Children of YHWH... I have highlighted a few but the whole book is powerful... Anyone having a true love for the Father will manifest this by their righteous conduct... It is impossible to truly please Him without knowing the commands pertaining to this conduct & abiding by them... The only way is through reading the scriptures daily & receiving The Holy Spirit given by YHWH... Yes at any stage of our Spiritual journey we will believe we love The Creator... but it is not the love with our whole heart, soul, mind & strength... because if it were we would no longer be living according to this fleshly world... We know we are of YHWH when we are walking in righteousness... All unrighteousness is sin... Those who are righteous are of YHWH & the rest are of the world are under the sway of the wicked one (1JOHN 5:19)... You cannot say you know YHWH if you are still enmeshed in the fleshly things of this world even if in your heart you truly believe you do... Following traditions & celebrations like Christmas, Easter, Valentine etc... having a desire for worldly status... envying what others have... putting importance on material things... is proof of still adhering to the things of the world (1 JOHN 2:16)... The evidence is that all those in the world who do not believe in YHWH & His Son follow these unrighteous ways & traditions... so then what would make us different from them... what sets us apart? Just believing is not enough... "Demons believe & shudder" — JAMES 2:19... True love & knowledge of YHWH The Father & His Son is not through saying but through doing... "He who says 'I know Him' & does not keep His Commandments is a liar & the Truth is not in him" — 1 JOHN 2:4... "Let us NOT love in word or in tongue... but in deed & in truth" — 1 JOHN 3:18...

Day 361: True Love is following YHWH's True Commands...

2 John 1; 3 John 1

Nearly all the church goers of today truly believe they are following the commands of The Father... but they are not... I know this from my own experience in my journey from wanting to know about the creation of this universe... to finding out that there is a Creator... to then at the time logically going to a church to find Him... to sitting on the church board and having a leadership position... to making a habit to reading The Scriptures which is now my daily routine... as breakfast is food for the body so The Word is food for my soul... to then really being given the wisdom of YHWH... to gaining the Truth of His Word... to sharing this with all those who say they are of Him... to then being shunned and rebuked by church leaders and some congregation members.. to me leaving and being free to live in YHWH's ultimate truth... True love for The Father and The Son is living emphatically to please them by inculcating Their Words in our heart... but you need to understand The Word because it is written in parables and only those who YHWH knows has a clean heart and away from idolatry can receive the wisdom and discernment necessary to walk according to The Word... When we truly love The Father and The Son then we have learnt to truly love others especially those who share the same Love of our Saviours...

Day 362: The Revelations of The Messiah...

Revelation 1, 2, 3, 4, 5

The last book of this bible & here I am reading the Revelations of John through the vision given by The Messiah & YHWH's Angel... The Messiah Yahsah is sitting on the Throne of YHWH & has provided His Throne to those who endure & overcome... He has opened the scroll with the 7 seals taken out of the Right Hand of YHWH... He is delivering the message of repentance to the 7 churches... "Fix up or lose your salvation"...

Day 363: Privilege & Power...

Revelation 6, 7, 8, 9, 10

It is truly a time of woe... but it is apparent very few can see this... The churches of today are succeeding in their mass deception & unfortunately the majority of the congregation have been fooled by the deception... I thank You Father YHWH Almighty for the privilege of knowing You... The One True El & Your Son my Messiah YAHSAH... The deception of Satan is huge & incredibly clever... You Father have given me intellectual power to see it & as a result salvation is mine... Church goers have been duped into believing these futile, superficial, man-made doctrines & that You have blessed them with the fleshly, materialistic things of this world... The world & the things in it has become so much more important to them... they have become so attached that they would rather hold onto to the temporary things than Your everlasting Spiritual gift... Father I am Yours... use me... The things of this world mean nothing to me except the beautiful children You gave me & all of those who are Yours... You loved the world so much you gave Your Son & what do they give in return? Superficial worship & a few moments when they can spare it... if they can spare it... What a displeasure man is to You... You do not deserve this... I will strive always to do Your will... exercising The Fruits of The Spirit always so I become better as a person & closer to You & my Messiah Yahsah... I love You Father... I love You my Messiah Yahsah... Amen... Amen... Amen!!!

Day 364: Babylon... who is she?

Revelation 12, 13, 14, 15, 16

Satan is the greatest deceiver... & he is indeed succeeding greatly in his biggest deception... His throne is in the church & he has successfully managed to deceive almost the whole world... those in the church & those outside... Babylon is the churches of today... on the high streets... on the corners... in the alleys... on the hills... in high & low places... in hot & cold climes... great & small... Everything I had known about the church has now been revealed as a lie... But only those of You Father will know & believe this... Your Word through The Holy Spirit has revealed the Truth to me...

Day 365: Amen!

Revelation 19, 20, 21, 22

And so shall it be… I have completed the The Holy Scriptures in one year as planned… I have kept my vow to YHWH… I have read The Word & relied solely on His Holy Spirit for interpretation… I delivered His message to those who needed to hear & read them… & now I am about to start the next phase of my journey with my Wonderful Father YHWH Almighty & my Beautiful Redeemer Yahsah The Messiah…It really doesn't matter what others may say or do that is in opposition concerning all that the Father has given me to minister…. I know YHWH is the Father & that Yahsah is His Son… I know as far as is possible right now I have Their Truth… & I know that it is this Truth that has indubitably set me free… free from the constraints of this fleshly, materialistic world & catapulted me in to the emancipated Spiritual realms with my Father… I am the most safest, contented, focused, grateful, powerful, humble, peaceful, joyous & loved I have ever been in my entire life & I have only my Father & my Messiah to thank for this through the Power of His Holy Spirit… May I rise to the challenge… May I be a pleasure to You… May I always listen to Your Voice & walk according to Your Righteous Commands… May I accept Your purpose for my life… May I never be afraid to speak Your Truth… I pray the whole world can see You as You truly are & give glory to You… YHWH Almighty… The Creator of this universe… The Father of He who gave His life to save ours… Yahsah The Messiah… The Lamb of the world…. The Alpha & The Omega… Amen!

Evidence of the Sanctification and Importance of the True Name of the Most High YAHWAH & of His Son YAHSAH the Messiah!

SPELLING, PRONUNCIATION & MEANING IN ENGLISH & HEBREW

YHWH — YaHWaH — יהוה (Yod... He... Vav... He) "He causes to become"

YHSH — YaHSaH — יהושע (Yod... He... Vav... Shin... Ayin) "YaH is salvation"

ACTS 4:12 "There is no other name under heaven given to man by which we are saved."

I CHRONICLES 16:8 "Give thanks to יהוה... call upon His Name... make known His deeds among the peoples."

PSALMS 83:18 "And let them know that You Whose Name is יהוה... You alone are the Most High over all the earth."

PSALMS 9:10 "And those who know Your name will put their trust in You... for You YHWH have not forsaken those who seek You."

ISAIAH 48:2 "They call themselves after the Holy City and lean on the El of Israel... יהוה of Hosts is His Name."

MATTHEW 1:21 "And you shall give birth to a Son and shall call His Name יהושע... for He shall save His People from their sins."

LUKE 2:21 "And when eight days were completed for Him to be circumcised His Name was called יהושע... the Name given by the messenger before He was conceived in the womb."

GENESIS

12:8 "Abraham built an altar to YHWH & called on the Name of YHWH."

26:25 "Abraham built an altar there & called on the Name of YHWH."

EXODUS

6:3 "I appeared to Abraham, Isaac & Jacob as El Shaddai... & by My Name YHWH was I not known to them."

9:16 "I have raised you up in order to show you My power & to declare My Name in all the Earth."

15:3 "YHWH is a Man of battle... YHWH is His Name."

20:7 "Do not take the Name of YHWH in vain."

20:24 "In every place where I cause My Name to be remembered I shall come to you & bless you."

23:21 "He is not going to pardon your transgressions for My Name is in Him."

33:19 "I shall proclaim the Name of YHWH before you."

34:5 "YHWH came down in the cloud... & proclaimed the Name YHWH."

LEVITICUS

18:21 "Do not profane the Name of El... I am YHWH."

19:12 "Do not swear falsely by YHWH's Name & so profane the Name of YHWH."

21:6 "They are holy to their El & do not profane the Name of YHWH."

22:32 "Do not profane My Holy Name."

24:16 "He who blasphemes the Name of YHWH shall be put to death."

NUMBERS

6:27 "They shall put My Name on the children of Israel & I shall bless them."

DEUTERONOMY

6:13 "Fear YHWH your El... serve Him & swear by His Name."

10:8 "YHWH separated the tribe of Levi... to bless in His Name to this day."

10:20 "Fear YHWH... serve Him... cling to Him & swear by his Name."

12:5 "But seek the place which YHWH chooses to put His Name."

12:11 "Unto the place which YHWH chooses to make His Name dwell."

14:24 "When the place where YHWH chooses to put His Name is too far."

18:5 "YHWH has chosen Levi to stand & serve in His Name..."

18:19 "The man who doesn't listen to My Words spoken in My Name."

28:10 "All the earth will see that the Name of YHWH is called on you."

28:58 "To fear the esteem Name of YHWH."

32:3 "I proclaim the Name of YHWH... ascribe greatness to our El."

RUTH

4:11 "Prove Your worth... & proclaim the Name in Bethlehem."

4:14 "Let His Name be proclaimed in Israel."

1 SAMUEL

12:22 "YHWH would not cast away His People for His Great Name Sake."

17:45 "I come to you in the Name of YHWH of Host."

20:42 "Go in peace since we have both sworn in the Name of YHWH."

2 SAMUEL

6:2 "To bring up the Ark of El that is called by the Name "YHWH of Hosts."

6:18 "When David finished offering he blessed them in the Name of YHWH."

7:13 "He does build a house for My Name."

7:26 "Let Your Name be made great forever… YHWH is El over Israel."

22:50 "I give thanks to you Oh YHWH… & sing praises to Your Name."

1 KINGS

3:2 "A House for the Name of YHWH had not been built until those days."

5:5 "Your son… he does build a house for My Name."

8:16 "I chose no city of Israel in which to build a House for My Name to be there but I chose David to be over My People."

8:29 "You said, My Name is there."

8:33 "When they've sinned & turned back to You to confess Your Name."

8:41 "A foreigner not of Your People who has come from afar for Your Name sake."

8:43 "All the people of the Earth will know Your Name & fear You & know the House that I built is called by Your Name."

10:1 "The Queen of Sheba heard of Solomon's report concerning YHWH's Name & came to question it hard."

11:36 "The city which I've chosen to put My Name there."

14:21 "Jerusalem… the city YHWH chose out of the Twelve Tribes to put His Name there."

18:24 "I shall call on the Name of YHWH."

18:32 "With the stones he built an altar in the Name of YHWH."

22:16 "Except you speak only the truth in the Name of YHWH."

2 KINGS

2:24 "He pronounced a curse on them in the Name of YHWH."

21:4 "YHWH said, 'In Jerusalem I put My Name.'"

2 CHRONICLES

20:9 "If evil does come upon us… such as the sword, judgment, pestilence or scarcity of food… We shall stand before this House and in Your presence… for Your Name is in this House… and cry out to You in our distress… & You do hear and save.'"

EZRA

6:12 "El… who has caused His Name to dwell there."

NEHEMIAH

1:9 "I will bring them to the place I have chosen to make My Name dwell there."

9:5 "Bless your El forever… Let them bless Your Holy Name."

9:10 "You made a Name for Yourself as it is this day."

JOB

1:21 "YHWH gives & He takes away… blessed be the Name of YHWH."

PSALMS

5:11 "Let those who love Your Name exult in You."

7:17 "I give thanks to YHWH & praise The Name of The Most High."

8:1 "Oh YHWH our Master… how excellent is Your Name in all the earth."

9:2 "I sing praise to Your Name oh Most High."

9:10 "Those who know Your Name trust in You."

18:49 "I give thanks to You YHWH… I sing praises to Your Name."

20:1 "The Name of the God of Jacob does set you on high."

20:5 "In the Name of our El we set up a banner."

20:7 "But we remember the Name of our God."

22:22 "I make known Your Name to My brothers... In the midst of the assembly I praise You."

23:3 "He turns back my being... He leads me in paths of righteousness for His Name's sake."

25:11 "For Your Name sake Oh YHWH You pardon my crookedness."

29:2 "Ascribe to YHWH the glory of His Name."

31:3 "You are my Rock... for Your Name sake lead me & guide me."

33:21 "For we have put our trust in His Holy Name."

34:3 "Make YHWH great with me & let's exult His Name together."

44:5 "Through Your Name we tread down those who rise up against us."

44:8 "In El we shall boast all day long & praise Your Name forever."

44:20 "If we have forgotten the Name of our El... would El not search this out."

45:17 "I cause Your Name to be remembered in all generations."

48:10 "According to Your Name... so is Your praise to the ends of the earth."

52: "In the presence of your kind ones I wait on Your Name... for it is good."

54:1 "Oh El, save me by Your Name."

54:6 "I praise Your Name Oh YHWH for it is good."

61:5 "You have given me the inheritance of those who fear Your Name."

61:8 "I sing praises to Your Name when I pay my vows daily."

63:4 "In Your Name I lift up my hands."

66:2 "Sing out the splendour of His Name."

66:4 "All the earth bow to You... they praise Your Name."

68:4 "Sing praises to His Name... by His Name Yah exult before Him."

68:18 "You have ascended on high… that Yah may dwell there."

69:30 "I praise the Name of YHWH with a song… & make Him great with thanksgiving."

69:36 "The seeds of His Servants will inherit Zion & those who love His Name shall dwell in it."

72:17 "Let His Name be blessed forever… let It continue before the sun."

72:19 "Blessed be His Esteem Name forever."

74:7 "They have profaned the dwelling place of Your Name to the ground."

74:10 "Would the enemy despise Your Name forever."

74:18 "A foolish people have despised Your Name."

74:21 "Let the poor & needy praise Your Name."

75:1 "We shall give thanks to YHWH… your Name is near."

76:1 "In Judah YHWH is known… His Name is great in Israel."

77:11 "I remember the deeds of YAH… Your wonders of old."

79:6 "Pour out your wrath on the nations who have not known You… and on reigns who have not called on Your Name."

79:9 "Help us for the sake of the esteem of Your Name… deliver us & cover our sins for Your Name sake."

80:18 "Revive us & let us call upon Your Name."

83:16 "Fill their faces with shame & let them seek Your Name oh YHWH."

83:18 "Let them know that You whose Name is YHWH is alone the Most High over all the Earth."

86:9 "Let the nations You have made bow down before You & esteem Your Name."

86:11 "Teach me Your Way… let me walk in Your Truth… unite my heart to fear Your Name."

86:12 "I praise You with all my heart Oh YHWH & I esteem Your Name forever."

89:8 “Oh YHWH… El of Host… Who is like You Oh Yah.”

89:12 “Tabor & Hermon rejoice in Your Name.”

89:16 “In Your Name they rejoice all day… exulted in Your Righteousness.”

89:24 “In My Name his horn is exulted.”

91:14 “I set him on high because he has known My Name.”

92:1 “Its good to give thanks to YHWH & to sing praises to Your Name.”

94:7 “They say ‘YAH does not see… The El of Jacob pays no heed.’”

96:2 “Sing to YHWH… bless His Name… proclaim His deliverance.”

96:8 “Ascribe to YHWH the glory of His Name.”

99:3 “They praise Your Name… great & awesome… It is Holy.”

99:6 “Samuel was among those calling on His Name.”

100:4 “Give thanks to Him… bless His Name.”

102:15 “The nations shall fear the Name of YHWH.”

102:21 “ To declare the Name of YHWH in Zion.”

103:1 “Bless YHWH Oh my being… bless His Holy Name.”

105:1 “Give thanks to YHWH… call upon His Name… make known His deeds among the People.”

105:3 “Make your boast in His Holy Name… let the hearts of those seeking YHWH rejoice.”

106:8 “He saved them for His Name sake to make His might known.”

106:47 “Save us Oh YHWH… to give thanks to Your Holy Name.”

109:21 “You Oh YHWH… deal with me for Your Name sake.”

111:9 “Holy & awesome is His Name.”

113:1 “Praise the Name of YHWH… Bless the Name of YHWH.”

115:1 “Not to us Oh YHWH but to Your Name give glory.”

116:4 “I called on the Name of YHWH… I pray to You… deliver my being.”

118:10 "The Gentiles surround me… In YHWH's Name I shall cut them off."

118:26 "Blessed is he who comes in the Name of YHWH."

119:55 "I remembered Your Name at night… I guard Your Law."

122:4 "Tribes of YaH… witnesses to Israel… to give thanks to the Name of YHWH."

124:8 "Our help is in the Name of YHWH… Maker of Heaven & Earth."

129:8 "They shall not say… 'We have blessed you in the Name of YHWH.'"

135:1 "Praise the Name of YHWH… praise you servants of YHWH."

135:3 "Praise YaH for He is good… sing praises to His Name for it is pleasant."

135:13 "YHWH Your Name is forever… Your remembrance to all generations."

138:2 "I give thanks to Your Name for Your kindness & truth… You have made great Your Word & Your Name above all."

140:13 "Let the righteous give thanks to Your Name… let the straight ones dwell in Your Presence."

142:7 "Bring my being out of prison to give thanks to Your Name."

143:11 "For the sake of Your Name Oh YHWH revive me."

145:1 "I exalt you Oh YHWH & bless Your Name forever & ever."

145:21 "My mouth speaks praise of YHWH… let all flesh bless His Holy Name."

148:5 "Let them Praise the Name of YHWH… He commanded & they were created."

149:3 "Let them praise His Name in a dance."

PROVERBS

18:10 "The Name of YHWH is a strong tower… the righteous run in it & are safe."

30:4 "What is His Name… & what is His Son's Name if you know."

ISAIAH

12:4 "In that day they'll say... 'Praise YHWH... call upon His Name... make known His deeds... make mention that His Name is exalted.'"

18:7 "To the place of the Name of YHWH of Hosts... to Mount Zion."

24:15 "Praise YHWH in the East... the Name of YHWH El of Israel in the coastlands."

25:1 "YHWH You are my El... I exult You... I praise Your Name... for You shall do wonders."

26:8 "The longing of our being is for Your Name & for the remembrance of You."

26:13 "Only in You do we make mention of Your Name."

29:23 "When Jacob sees his children... the work of My hands... they shall set apart My Name and set apart the Holy One of Jacob."

30:27 "The Name of **יהוה** is coming from afar burning with His wrath and heavy smoke."

41:25 "I have stirred up one from the north and he comes... from the rising of the sun he calls on My Name."

42:8 "I am **יהוה**... that is My Name... and My glory I do not give to another... nor My praise to idols."

43:7 "All those who are called by My Name... whom I have created... formed... even made for My glory"

47:4 "Our Redeemer... **יהוה** of hosts is His Name... the Holy One of Israel."

48:1 "Hear this house of Jacob... called by the name of Israel... who swear by the Name of **יהוה** though not in truth or in righteousness."

48:2 "They call themselves after the holy city and lean on the El of Israel... **יהוה** of hosts is His Name."

49:1 "Listen to Me and hear peoples from afar... **יהוה** has called Me from the womb... from My mother's belly He has caused My Name to be remembered."

50:10 "Who among you is fearing יהוה... obeying the voice of His Servant... that has walked in darkness and has no light? Let him trust in the Name of יהוה."

51:15 "But I am יהוה your El stirring up the sea and its waves roar... יהוה of hosts is His Name."

52:6 "Therefore My people shall know My Name... for I am the One who is speaking... See... it is I."

54:5 "For your Maker is your husband... יהוה of hosts is His Name and the Holy One of Yisra'ěl is your Redeemer... He is called the El of all the earth."

56:6 "Also the sons of the foreigner who join themselves to יהוה... to serve Him and to love the Name of יהוה... to be His servants... all who guard the Sabbath."

57:15 "For thus declares the high and exalted One who dwells forever... whose Name is Holy."

59:19 "They shall fear the Name of יהוה from the west and His glory from the rising of the sun."

63:14 "As a beast goes down into the valley and the Spirit of יהוה causes him to rest... so You led Your people to make Yourself a comely Name."

63:16 "You are our Father though Abraham does not know us and Yisra'ěl does not recognise us... You O יהוה are our Father... our Redeemer... Your Name is from of old."

64:2 "To make Your Name known to Your adversaries so that nations tremble before You."

66:5 "Hear the Word of יהוה you who tremble at His Word... Your brothers who hate you... who cast you out for My Name's sake said... 'Let יהוה be esteemed.'"

JEREMIAH

3:17 "At that time Yerushalayim shall be called the throne of יהוה... and all the nations shall be gathered to the Name of יהוה to Yerushalayim."

7:10 "And you came and stood before Me in this house which is called by My Name & said... 'We have been delivered in order to do all these abominations."

7:30 "'The children of Yehudah have done what is evil in My eyes' declares יהוה... 'They have set abominations in the house which is called by My Name.'"

10:6 "There is none like You O יהוה... You are great & great is Your Name in might."

10:16 "The Portion of Ya'aqob is not like these... for He is the Maker of all and Yisra'ěl is the tribe of His inheritance... יהוה of hosts is His Name."

11:21 "Therefore thus said יהוה 'Do not prophesy in the Name of יהוה lest you die by our hand.'"

12:16 "If they learn well the ways of My people... to swear by My Name... 'As יהוה lives'... then they shall be established in the midst of My people."

14:7 "O יהוה though our crookedness's witness against us... act for Your Name's sake."

15:16 "Your words were found & I ate them... Your word was to me the joy & rejoicing of my heart... for Your Name is called on me O יהוה El of hosts."

16:21 "Therefore I am causing them to know My hand and My might... and they shall know that My Name is יהוה!"

31:35 "Thus said יהוה who gives the sun for a light by day and the laws of the moon and the stars for a light by night... who stirs up the sea and its waves roar... יהוה of hosts is His Name."

32:18 "You show kindness to thousands and repay the crookedness of the fathers into the bosom of their children... The Great... The Mighty Ěl... יהוה of hosts is His Name."

33:2 "Thus said יהוה who made it... יהוה who formed it to establish it... יהוה is His Name."

44:26 "Hear the word of יהוה all Judah dwelling in Mitsrayim... 'I have sworn by My Great Name... My Name shall no longer be called upon by the mouth of any man of Judah in the land of Mitsrayim saying... "As the Master יהוה lives."

46:18 "'As I live' declares the Sovereign whose Name is יהוה of Hosts... 'For as Tabor is among the mountains and as Karmel by the sea He shall come."

48:15 "'Mo'ab is ravaged... her cities entered... her chosen young men gone down to slaughter' declares the Sovereign whose Name is יהוה of Hosts."

50:34 "Their Redeemer is strong... יהוה of hosts is His Name... He shall strongly plead their case giving rest to the land but unrest to the inhabitants of Babel."

51:19 "The Portion of Ya'aqob is not like them... for He is the Maker of all & Yisra'ěl is the tribe of His inheritance... יהוה of hosts is His Name."

LAMENTATION

3:55 "I called on Your Name O יהוה from the lowest pit."

EZEKIEL

20:14 "But I acted for My Name's sake not to profane it before the gentiles... before whose eyes I had brought them out."

36:23 "I shall set apart My great Name which has been profaned... & the gentiles shall know that I am יהוה when I'm set-apart in you before their eyes."

39:7 "And I shall make My Holy Name known in the midst of My people Yisra'ěl and not let My Holy Name be profaned anymore... and the gentiles shall know that I am יהוה The Holy One in Yisra'ěl."

43:7 "Son of man… this is the place of My throne… the place of the soles of My feet… when I dwell in the midst of the children of Yisra'ěl forever… and the house of Yisra'ěl shall no longer defile My Holy Name."

48:35 "All around… eighteen thousand cubits… and the name of the city from that day is 'יהוה is there'!"

DANIEL

9:6 "We did not listen to Your servants the prophets who spoke in Your Name to our sovereigns, our heads, and our fathers & to the people of the land."

JOEL

2:26 "You shall eat & be satisfied and praise the Name of יהוה your El who has done with you so wondrously… My people shall never be put to shame."

2:32 "And it shall be that everyone who calls on the Name of יהוה shall be delivered… for on Mount Tsiyon and in Yerushalayim there shall be an escape as יהוה has said and among the survivors whom יהוה calls."

AMOS

4:13 "He who forms mountains… creates the wind… who declares to man what his thought is… makes the morning darkness and who treads the high places of the earth… יהוה El of hosts is His Name."

5:8 "He who made Pleiades and Orion… who turns the shadow of death into morning and darkened day into night… who is calling for the waters of the sea and pours them out on the face of the earth… יהוה is His Name."

6:10 "If a relative or his undertaker brings the remains out of the house… he shall say to one inside the house… 'Is anyone with you?' and he says 'No'… then he shall say 'Hush!'… for we have not remembered the Name of יהוה!"

9:6 "Who is building His upper room in the heavens and has founded His firmament on the earth... Who is calling for the waters of the sea and pours them out on the face of the earth? **יהוה** is His Name."

MICAH

4:5 "For all the peoples walk... each one in the name of his mighty one... But we walk in the Name of **יהוה** our El forever and ever."

5:4 "And He shall stand and shepherd in the strength of **יהוה**, in the excellency of the Name of **יהוה** His Elohim. And they shall dwell... for at that time He shall be great to the ends of the earth."

ZEPHANIAH

3:9 "For then I shall turn unto the peoples a clean lip so that they all call on the Name of **יהוה**... to serve Him with one shoulder."

ZECHARIAH

4:6 "And he answered and said to me, 'This is the word of **יהוה** to Zerubbabel, 'Not by might... nor by power... but by My Spirit' said **יהוה** of hosts."

5:4 "'I shall send it out' declares **יהוה** of hosts... 'and it shall come into the house of the thief... the one swearing falsely by My Name.... and it shall remain in the midst of his house and shall consume it'."

10:12 "'And I shall make them mighty in **יהוה**... so that they walk up and down in His Name' declares **יהוה**."

13:9 "And I shall bring the third into fire and refine them as silver is refined... and try them as gold is tried.... they shall call on My Name and I shall answer them... I shall say... This is My people' while they say... '**יהוה** is my Elohim'."

14:9 "And **יהוה** shall be Sovereign over all the earth... in that day there shall be one **יהוה** and His Named One."

MALACHI

1:6 "A son esteems his father… & a servant his master… 'If I am the Father where is My esteem… If I am a Master where is My fear?' said יהוה to you priests who despise My Name… but you asked… In what way have we despised Your Name?'"

1:11 "'For from the rising of the sun even to its going down… My Name is great among nations… and in every place incense is presented to My Name and a clean offering… for My Name is great among nations' said יהוה of hosts."

2:1 "'And now O priests… this command is for you… "If you do not hear and if you do not take it to heart to give esteem to My Name' said יהוה of hosts… 'I shall send a curse upon you… and I shall curse your blessings…. and indeed I have cursed them because you do not take it to heart."

3:16 "Then shall those who fear יהוה speak to one another… and יהוה listen and hear… and a book of remembrance be written before Him… of those who fear יהוה and those who think upon His Name."

4:2 "To you who fear My Name the Sun of Righteousness shall arise with healing in His wing… & you shall go out leaping for joy like calves from the stall."

MATTHEW

21:9 "The crowds who went before and followed cried out… 'Hosanna in the highest to the Son of David… blessed is He who comes in the Name of יהוה."

23:39 "'I say to you from now on you shall by no means see Me until you say 'Blessed is He who is coming in the Name of יהוה!'"

LUKE

2:21 "And when eight days were completed for Him to be circumcised His Name was called יהושע... the Name given by the messenger before He was conceived in the womb."

13:35 "See... your House is left to you laid waste... And truly I say to you... you shall by no means see Me until the time comes when you say... 'Blessed is He who is coming in the Name of יהוה'!"

JOHN

1:12 "But as many as received Him to them He gave the authority to become children of El... to those believing in His Name."

3:18 "He who believes in Him isn't judged... but he who doesn't is judged because he hasn't believed in the Name of the only begotten Son of El."

5:43 "I have come in My Father's Name and you do not receive Me... If another comes in his own name him you would receive."

ACTS

2:21 "It shall be that everyone who calls on the Name of יהוה shall be saved.'"

4:12 "There is no deliverance in anyone else... for there is no other Name under the heaven given among men by which we need to be saved."

10:43 "To this One all the prophets bear witness that through His Name everyone believing in Him does receive forgiveness of sins."

1 CORINTHIANS

6:11 "Such were some of you... but you were washed... you were set apart... you were declared right in the Name of the Master יהושע and by the Spirit of YHWH."

JAMES

5:10 "My brothers… as an example of suffering and patience… take the prophets who spoke in the Name of יהוה."

1 JOHN

3:23 "And this is His command that we should believe in the Name of His Son יהושע Messiah and love one another as He gave us command."

The Trinity:

Mystery... Mistake... or Malediction? Fact or Falsehood?

ROMANS 10:9 proclaims: "If you confess with your mouth the Master Yahsah and believe in your heart that YHWH raised Him from the dead then you shall be saved."

JOHN 3:16 declares: "YHWH so loved the world He gave His Only Begotten Son… that everyone exercising faith in Him should not perish but possess everlasting life."

JOHN 3:35 asserts: "The Father loves The Son."

PSALMS 110:1 affirms: "YHWH said to my Master… 'Sit at My Right Hand until I make Your enemies a footstool for Your Feet"

LUKE 23:46 documents: "Crying out with a loud voice **יהושע** said… 'Father into Your Hands I commit My Spirit".

I remember when I first started to doubt the trinity… & it was no wonder… in asking my pastor to help give me understanding of this confusing doctrine he persisted in trying to make me believe that YHWH The Father was Yahsah The Messiah as The Son who came down to earth in the flesh… When this explanation still didn't make sense to me he would then say… "It's a mystery"… It's no mystery… what it is is an erroneous & ludicrous doctrine devised to deceive the masses on a global scale… The Gospel of JOHN clearly states a distinction between The Father & The Son… It is a serious misconception to believe in the trinitarian doctrine & accept it as a mystery…

JOHN 3:33 states: "He who has received His testimony has certified that YHWH is true."

YHWH reveals all His Sacred Secrets & mysteries to His Children… why would He want to hide them?

MARK 4:11 emphasises: "To you it has been given to know the mystery of The Kingdom of YHWH… But to those on the outside everything is in parables unless they should turn back & their sins be forgiven"…

YHWH Almighty has no hidden secrets from His Children… He is The Father & Yahsah The Messiah is His Son… We follow The Messiah as an example of true obedience… In order to be obedient we need someone or something to obey… That was why He came down to earth… He obeyed His Father… & we obey Him… This is the world's only hope of salvation!

Below is a list of Holy Scriptures that refute the trinitarian doctrine and upholds The Father YHWH & His Beloved Son Yahsah as separate Spiritual entities:

PSALMS

45:2 "You are more handsome than the sons of men… favour has been poured upon Your lips… therefore YHWH has blessed You forever."

110:1 "YHWH said to my Master… 'Sit at My Right Hand until I make Your enemies a footstool for Your feet.'"

PROVERBS

30:4 "Who has gone up to the heavens and come down? Who has gathered the wind in His fists? Who has bound the waters in a garment? Who established all the ends of the earth? What is His Name… & what is His Son's Name… if you know it?"

ISAIAH

49:1-6 "Listen to Me O coastlands… and hear you peoples from afar! **יהוה** has called Me from the womb… from My mother's belly He has caused My Name to be remembered…. & He made My mouth like a sharp sword… In the shadow of His hand He hid Me and made Me a polished shaft… In His quiver He hid Me & He said to Me… 'You are My Servant O Israel in whom I am adorned.' And I said… 'I have laboured in vain… I have spent my strength for emptiness and in vain… but my right-ruling is with יהוה and my work with my Elohim.'" "And now" said יהוה — who formed Me from the womb to be His Servant… to bring Jacob back to Him though Israel is not gathered to Him… yet I am esteemed in the eyes of יהוה & My Elohim has been My strength… And He says… "Shall it be a small matter for You to be My Servant to raise up the tribes of Jacob and to bring back the preserved ones of Israel? And I shall give You as a light to the gentiles to be My deliverance to the ends of the earth!"

50:4-10 "The Master יהוה has given Me the tongue of taught ones that I should know to help the weary with a word… He wakes Me morning by morning… He wakes My ear to hear as taught ones…. The Master יהוה has opened My ear and I was not rebellious nor did I turn away… I gave My back to those who struck Me and My cheeks to those who plucked out the beard… I did not hide My face from humiliation and spitting… & the Master יהוה helps Me… Therefore I shall not be humiliated… so I have set My face like a flint and I know that I am not put to shame… Near is He who declares Me right… Who would contend with Me? Let us stand together… Who is My adversary? Let him come near Me… See the Master יהוה helps Me… Who would declare Me wrong? See all of them wear out like a garment… a moth eats them… Who among you is fearing יהוה… obeying the voice of His Servant that has walked in darkness and has no light? Let him trust in the Name of יהוה and lean upon his Elohim!"

DANIEL

7:13-14 "I was looking in the night visions and saw One like the Son of Enoch coming with the clouds of the heavens! And He came to the Ancient of Days and they brought Him near before Him… & to Him was given rulership and preciousness and a reign… that all peoples, nations and languages should serve Him… His rule is an everlasting rule which shall not pass away… & His reign that which shall not be destroyed."

MICAH

5:2, 4 "But you Bethlehem Ephrathah... You who are little among the clans of Judah... Out of you shall come forth to Me the One to become Ruler in Israel... & His comings forth are of old... from everlasting... & He shall stand and shepherd in the strength of יהוה... in the excellency of the Name of יהוה His Elohim... & they shall dwell... for at that time He shall be great to the ends of the earth."

MATTHEW

3:17 "See a voice out of the heavens saying... 'This is My Son the Beloved in whom I do delight.'"

10:32 "Everyone therefore who shall confess Me before men... him I shall also confess before My Father who is in the heavens."

10:40 "He who receives you receives Me... and he who receives Me receives Him who sent Me."

11:27 "All have been handed over to Me by My Father... no one knows the Son except the Father... nor does anyone know the Father except the Son."

12:32 "Anyone who speaks a word against the Son of Man it will be forgiven him... but whoever speaks against the Holy Spirit it will not be forgiven him... either in this age or in the age to come."

16:17 "יהושע answering said to him... 'Blessed are you Peter for flesh and blood has not revealed this to you but My Father in the heavens.'"

19:17 "He said... 'Why do you call Me good? No one is good except One... YHWH... but if you wish to enter into life guard The Commands.'"

20:23 "So He said to them... 'You will indeed drink My cup & be baptised with the baptism that I am baptised with... but to sit on My right Hand & on My left is not Mine to give but it is for those for whom it is prepared by My Father.'"

25:34 "Then the Sovereign shall say to those on His right Hand… 'Come you blessed of My Father… inherit the reign prepared for you from the foundation of the world.'"

26:39 "He fell on His face and prayed saying… 'O My Father… if it is possible let this cup pass from Me… yet not as I desire but as You desire.'"

28:18 "יהושע came up and spoke to them saying… 'All authority has been given to Me in heaven and on earth.'"

MARK

9:7 "This is My Beloved Son… hear Him."

9:37 "Whoever receives one of such little children in My Name receives Me… and whoever receives Me receives not Me but the One who sent Me."

13:32 "No one knows except The Father… not even The Son."

14:36 "And He said… 'Abba… Father… all is possible for You… make this cup pass from Me… yet not what I desire but what You desire.'"

16:19 "Then indeed after the Master had spoken to them He was received up into the heaven and sat down at the right hand of YHWH."

LUKE

12:10 "Everyone who shall speak a word against the Son of Adam it shall be forgiven him… but to him who has blasphemed against the Holy Spirit it shall not be forgiven."

22:42 "Father if it be Your Counsel remove this cup from Me… yet not My desire but let Yours be done."

23:46 "Crying out with a loud voice **יהושע** said… 'Father into Your Hands I commit My Spirit'."

JOHN

3:35 "The Father loves the Son and has given all into His hand."

5:17 "But יהושע answered them… "My Father works until now… and I work."

5:30 "Of Myself I am unable to do any matter… As I hear I judge & My judgment is righteous because I do not seek My own desire but the desire of the Father who sent Me."

6:38 "I have come down out of the heaven not to do My own desire but the desire of Him Who sent Me."

7:16 "Yahsah answered them & said… 'My teaching is not Mine but His Who sent Me.'"

7:33 "Therefore יהושע said to them… 'Yet a little while I am with you… then I go to Him Who sent Me.'"

8:17,18 "In your Law it has been written that the witness of two men is true… I am One who witnesses concerning Myself… and the Father who sent Me witnesses concerning Me."

10:17 "Because of this the Father loves Me… because I lay down My life in order to receive it again."

12:28 "Father esteem Your Name"… then a voice came from the heaven… 'I have both esteemed it and shall esteem it again.'"

13:16 "He Who is sent is not greater than He Who sent Him."

13:20 "He who receives who I send receives Me… He who receives Me receives My Father."

14:21 "He who possesses My commands and guards them it is he who loves Me… and He who loves Me shall be loved by My Father… & I shall love him and manifest Myself to him."

14:24 "He who does not love Me does not guard My Words… & the Word which you hear are not mine but of the Father Who sent Me."

14:28 "You heard that I said to you I am going away and I am coming to you… if you did love Me you would have rejoiced that I said I am going to The Father… for The Father is greater than I."

14:31 "But in order for the world to know that I love the Father & that as the Father commanded Me... so I am doing."

15:10 "If you guard My commands you shall stay in My love even as I have guarded My Father's Command & stay in His Love."

15:15 "No longer do I call you servants for a servant does not know what his master is doing... but I have called you friends... for all teachings which I heard from My Father I have made known to you."

16:5 "But now I go away to Him who sent Me."

16:28 "I came forth from the Father & have come into the world... again I leave the world to go to The Father."

Chapter 17 READ ALL

17:11 "I am no more in the world but these are in the world... & I come to You Holy Father... Guard them in Your Name which You have given Me so that they might be one as We are."

17:20-23 "I do not pray for these alone but also for those believing in Me through their word... so that they all might be one as You Father are in Me and I in You... so that they too might be one in Us so that the world might believe that You have sent Me... & the glory which You gave Me I have given to them so that they might be one as We are One... I in them and You in Me so that they might be perfected into one... so that the world knows that You have sent Me & have loved them as You have loved Me."

20:17 "Yahsah said to her... 'Do not hold on to Me for I have not yet ascended to My Father... but go to My brothers & say to them I am ascending to My Father & your Father... & to My El and your El."

ACTS

2:36 "Therefore let all the house of Israel know for certain that YHWH has made this **יהושע** whom you impaled both Master and Messiah."

3:13 "The El of Abraham, Isaac & Jacob glorified His Servant **יהושע** whom you delivered up and denied in the presence of Pilate."

3:15 "But you killed the Leader of life... Whom YHWH raised from the dead of which we are witnesses."

4:26 "The sovereigns of the earth stood up & the rulers were gathered together against יהוה and against His Messiah... for truly they were gathered together against Your Holy Servant יהושע whom You anointed."

7:55,56 "But he being filled with the Holy Spirit looked steadily into the heaven and saw the glory of יהוה and יהושע standing at His Right Hand... and he said... "Look! I see the heavens opened and the Son of Adam standing at the Right Hand of YHWH!"

10:38,40 "YHWH did anoint Yahsah of Nazareth with the Holy Spirit & with power... Who went about doing good & healing all who were oppressed by the devil... for YHWH was with Him... YHWH raised up This One on the third day & let Him be seen."

10:42 "He commanded us to proclaim to the people & to witness that it is He Who was appointed by YHWH to be Judge of the living & the dead."

13:33 "Having raised up Yahsah as it is written in the 2nd Psalms... 'You are my Son... today I have brought You forth."

17:31 "He has set a day on which He is going to judge the world in righteousness by a Man Whom He has appointed... having given proof of this to all by raising Him from the dead."

ROMANS

10:9-10 "If you confess with your mouth the Master יהושע and believe in your heart that YHWH has raised Him from the dead you shall be saved... for with the heart one believes unto righteousness & one confesses with the mouth... & so is saved."

4:24 "Righteousness imputed to those who believe in Him who raised Yahsah from the dead."

5:10 "For if being enemies we were restored to favour with YHWH through the death of His Son… much more having been restored to favour we shall be saved by His life."

6:4 "We were therefore buried with Him through baptism into death that as Yahsah was raised from the dead by the glory of The Father so also we should walk in newness of life."

8:9 "But you are not in the flesh but in the Spirit if indeed the Spirit of YHWH dwells in you… & if anyone does not have the Spirit of Yahsah this one is not His."

8:17 "If children then also Heirs… truly Heirs of YHWH & joint Heirs with The Messiah… if indeed we suffer with Him in order that we also be exalted together."

1 CORINTHIANS

3:23 "You belong to Yahsah… & Yahsah belongs to YHWH."

15:28 "When all are made subject to Him then the Son Himself shall also be subject to Him Who put all under Him in order that YHWH be all in all."

2 CORINTHIANS

5:21 "He made Him who knew no sin to be sin for us so that in Him we might become the righteousness of YHWH."

GALATIANS

1:1 "Paul an apostle… not from men… nor by a man… but by **יהושע** Messiah and YHWH the Father who raised Him from the dead."

EPHESIANS

1:20, 22 "He raised Yahsah from the dead & seated Him at His Right Hand in the heavens… & He put all things under His feet & gave Him to be head over all."

4:5,6 "One Master… one faith… one baptism… One El & Father of all… Who is above all… & through all… & in you all."

COLOSSIANS

3:1 "If then you were raised with Yahsah The Messiah seek the matters which are above where Yahsah is sitting at the right hand of YHWH."

1 THESSALONIANS

1:10 "Wait for His Son from the heavens Whom He raised from the dead… Yahsah Who is delivering us from the wrath to come."

1 TIMOTHY

2:5 "For there is one El & one Mediator between YHWH & men… The Messiah Yahsah."

1 PETER

1:21 "YHWH raised Him from the dead & gave Him glory so that your belief & hope are in YHWH."

3:22 "Having gone into the heaven Yahsah is at the Right Hand of YHWH… angels, authority & powers having been subjected to Him."

2 PETER

1:17 "For when He received respect & glory from YHWH the Father such a voice came to Him from the Excellent Esteem… 'This is My Son The Beloved in whom I delight.'"

HEBREWS

Chapter 1 READ ALL

5:5 "So also the Messiah did not extol Himself to become High Priest but it was He who said to Him, 'You are My Son… today I have brought You forth."

5:7 "As He also says in another place... 'You are a priest forever according to the order of Malchizedek'... who in the days of His flesh when He had offered up prayers & petitions with strong crying & tears to Him who was able to save Him from death & was heard because of His reverent fear... though being a Son He learned obedience by what He suffered... & having been perfected He became the Causer of everlasting deliverance to all those obeying Him."

8:1,2 "Now the summary of what we are saying is... We have such a High Priest who is seated at the right hand of the throne of the Greatness in the heavens & who serves in the Holy Place... of the true Tent which YHWH set up & not man."

8:6 "Now He has obtained a more excellent service inasmuch as He is also Mediator of a better covenant which was constituted on better promises."

9:24 "For Yahsah has not entered into a Holy Place made by hand but into the heaven itself to appear in the presence of YHWH on our behalf."

10:7 "Then I said... 'See I come... in the roll of the book it has been written concerning Me... to do Your desire O Elohim."

1 JOHN

5:1 "Everyone who believes that Yahsah is The Messiah has been born of YHWH... & everyone who loves the One bringing forth also loves the One having been born of Him."

REVELATION

1:6 "He has made us kings & priests to His Elohim & Father... to Him be the glory & rule forever & ever."

3:21 "To him who overcomes I shall give to sit with Me on My throne as I also overcame and sat down with My Father on His throne."

5:7 "Then He came & took the scroll out of the Hand of Him sitting on the throne."

References

1. The Scriptures 2009: The Institute for Scripture Research 1993-2015

2. The Holy Bible; New King James Version; Thomas Nelson 1982

3. The Holy Word of YHWH (Unpublished); A Noble healed by El 2003

“Let everything that breathes praise YaH!”

PSALMS 150:6

www.ingramcontent.com/pod-product-compliance
Ingram Content Group UK Ltd.
Pitfield, Milton Keynes, MK11 3LW, UK
UKHW021827270726
14058UKWH00001B/20